THAT REMINDS ME

A Conversational Memoir

Norman Zierold

Anapurna Press
Fairfield, Iowa, USA

That Reminds Me

For information contact:

Norman Zierold
1105 Granville Avenue
Fairfield, Iowa 52556
641-470-1313

email: nzierold@mum.edu

or visit: www.NormanZierold.WordPress.com

ISBN-13:   978-0-9792104-4-0

ISBN-10:   0-9792104-4-5

First printing: 2013

Second printing: 2013

Cover design by George Foster
Front cover photo by Mary Drew
Interior design by Allen Cobb

Anapurna Press
Fairfield, Iowa, USA

www.anapurnaPress.com

Praise for THAT REMINDS ME

"What a creative and entertaining way to tell a story of a life and a time! Congratulations, Norman—a thoroughly enjoyable and informative read."

—David Lynch, Filmmaker

"I very much enjoyed reading your book and devoured it much faster than I did many another. Thank you for writing it."

—John Simon, Critic of the Arts

"Cheers for Norman Zierold who has written a memoir that is charming, touching, and—real real!"

—Sidney Offit, author of *Memoir of the Bookie's Son*

"When you read *That Reminds Me* you will meet and love Norman Zierold, clearly an extraordinary man with a pure heart, incisive wit, deep insights into universal truths—and one of the finest storytellers in the land. I read the book in a single record-breaking session. Blissful!"

—Bob Roth, Executive Director, David Lynch Foundation

"I just finished *That Reminds Me* and the author accomplished what I have been hoping for over many years. He has seamlessly woven a message of real wisdom into the fabric of a life of significant material interest. This is a book where I feel I really connected with the author's humanity; it was as if he had been sitting in my room all week chatting with me. That is a rarity for me to find."

—Craig Berg, author of *That's a Great Story*

"I loved your book, every aspect of it—the stories, the people, the life questions, the intimate and appreciative asides to the reader. If your book had nine hundred pages, I would still be enjoying it, as my breakfast companion every morning."

—Burton Milward, Jr., author of *The Sun Salutation Exercise (Surya Namaskara)*

"It's a privilege to sit down with someone who has lived a full life, with wisdom and life's lessons learned, somehow reminiscent of Forrest Gump, all told in a whimsical style that leaves you chuckling throughout. I highly recommend it."

—Ken Chawkin, Publicist, Producer, Poet

"Unputdownable! I love this book. It is funny, full of interesting stories, and touching and satisfying as the author discusses how he fulfilled his spiritual quests. I don't recommend starting to read it late in the evening because you may never go to bed that night."

—Toni Alazraki, Educator and Humorist

Other Books by Norman Zierold

The Child Stars

Little Charlie Ross

Three Sisters in Black
(Recipient of a Special Edgar Allen Poe Award)

The Moguls

Garbo

The Skyscraper Doom

Sex Goddesses of the Silent Screen

Contents

Foreword

No need to fasten your safety belts, as Bette Davis famously advised in the film *All About Eve*. You're not in for the "bumpy ride" she forecast. Instead, the memoir you're about to dive into promises to be a smooth and refreshing ride.

Rather than a chronology of his life, the author offers you an engaging conversation interlaced with fascinating facts, colorful characters, and a plethora of laughs.

You'll hear about his sunny childhood in the utopian Amana Colonies of Iowa and his extraordinary years studying and working with famed Indian sage Maharishi Mahesh Yogi. While spiritual aspirations thrive, equal time goes to worldly realms, where more aspects of the visionary Utopia surface. Which strand gains the upper hand in this cheerful, revealing autobiography? The answer may be a pleasant surprise.

You'll savor his versatile writing career in the midst of the glitterati of Hollywood and New York, among them, Barbara Walters, Andy Warhol, Shelley Winters, Anthony Quinn, Mae West, Groucho Marx, Roddy McDowall, Jackie Coogan, Rex Harrison, and many more.

On foreign terrain, you'll encounter a president of France, as well as the greatly gifted composer Francis Poulenc. Back home among literati, you'll catch telling glimpses of celebrated diarist Anaïs Nin, Tennessee Williams, E.E. Cummings, and pixyish poet Dylan Thomas.

You'll become privy to a cornucopia of tastes, eccentricities, and opinions, some orthodox, others outrageous. Whether you agree with them or not, it's doubtful you'll be bored by this spontaneous account of a variegated and satisfying life.

All right then, ready for lift-off? Enjoy!

Fairfield, Iowa, USA
January 12, 2013

1. Anecdotes Galore

Years ago I read that the perfect start of a story would be "'Take your hand off my knee!' said the Duchess." I liked the idea so much that I sat right down and used it. Now I'm in a similar spot, looking for a brisk beginning for this unconventional memoir. Well, here it is, whisking you right into my heart and mind. We're off to the theatre!

When the Broadway musical *Wonderful Town* was revived a while back I was reminded of the play it was based on, *My Sister Eileen*, which debuted in the 1940s with me in the theatre, applauding eagerly, especially when it came to my favorite line. In the plot, two young sisters forsake Ohio to try and make it in New York. They find a Greenwich Village apartment to which one evening come their double dates. Everyone tries to make conversation but everything falls flat. Desperate, Eileen breaks the embarrassing silence with her best gambit. "I was rereading *Moby Dick* last night," she gamely begins — and gets the biggest laugh of the evening.

Somehow this reminds me of Martin Luther's line, "I cannot and will not read Kant." Well, that's what I thought a radio evangelist was saying, quite a reasonable sentiment, it seemed to me, who find most philosophers a bit windy, until a friend explained that what Martin said was, "I cannot and will not recant." Of course Luther could hardly have been speaking of Kant, who was not yet born, and who in due course said something I have long cherished — "Two things fill me with ever increasing wonder, the starry skies above me and the moral law within me." "Starry skies" reminds me of blue skies.

Naturally, Irving Berlin's *Blue Skies* comes to mind but that, for the moment, will have to give way to Martin Luther's constipation, which came to mind a split second earlier. Luther shared this affliction with many other great figures, among them Abraham Lincoln and Napoleon Bonaparte. "Honest Abe" was lucky to have one bowel movement a week and then only with the aid of blue mass, a common remedy of the time, so-called because finely divided mercury gave the pill a blue cast. As for Napoleon, while in exile on Saint Helena he spoke of this chronic ailment and declared his "heroic remedy" for it to be "soupe à la reine," made up of milk, egg yolk, and sugar. Luther's laxative does not come to mind but blue mass naturally brings back *Blue Skies*. As you will see, I'm fond of background stories about pop classics.

In late 1926, Broadway headliner Belle Baker called Irving Berlin and asked him to come to the rescue of her new show, *Betsy*, about to open. Berlin went to his trunk and pulled out an unfinished song that he felt had possibilities. In a marathon all-night session, with some help from Belle and her husband, he completed *Blue Skies*. As Belle feared, her show debuted to a dismal reception — until near the end when she sang *Blue Skies*. The audience was galvanized by the sweet simple tune and demanded no less than 23 encores!

So say the historic accounts, which to me seem suspect. Yes, it's a simple, lovely tune — but 23 encores! That might have inflicted permanent brain damage, no? In any event, by that time the emotionally charged and drained Belle forgot the lyric. Berlin, in the first row, got up and joined her for a final version to tumultuous applause. As the not so very old saying goes, "There's no business like show business."

The song by that name seems to have been around forever but actually made its Broadway debut in *Annie Get Your Gun*, in 1945. I was 18 at the time, in a navy uniform, and lucky to get a seat in the second balcony, the last row of the second balcony, to be precise. The distant location didn't matter because the great Ethel Merman starred and her clarion delivery carried to the rafters.

Along with her splendid voice, Ethel had a sense of humor. In her autobiography she referred to several husbands, including actor Ernest Borgnine, to whom she devoted a chapter with but a single page and that page she left — virgin white!

What is left unsaid can sometimes be quite telling. Over the years spent in the company of my mother I never — literally never — heard her speak of her parents. Finally one day I asked her why. "Not much to say," she replied. And that was that.

Which reminds me of the old Vedantic formula — "I am That, You are That, This is That, and That is That!" Well, let's call it a variation on the old Vedic formula. On the title page of a *Guru Gita* I once bought second hand someone had written, "I Dat, You Dat, Dis Dat, Dat Dat."

"Second hand" recalls another song I admire, *Second Hand Rose*, especially when sung by the inimitable Fanny Brice, the inspiration for the musical *Funny Girl*. I love the story about her where she's asked if she speaks French, to which she replies, "No, I always believed in just speaking one language good."

But back to "Dat Dat," which was someone's way of describing the absolute, or a state of unboundedness, something I first experienced a quarter of a century ago, and then, remarkable though it was, in an easy spontaneous flow. It was during a Transcendental Meditation® course called "A Taste of Utopia" in Fairfield, Iowa, in 1983. Responding to a call from Maharishi Mahesh Yogi, over eight thousand meditators from around the world gathered for three weeks of group practice to prove that numbers like that could change the trends of time for the better.

As predicted by participating scientists, a global wave of harmony and goodwill ensued, three weeks of significant progress toward peace along with declines in negative sectors such as crime, traffic accidents, and infectious diseases. Once the assembly ended, each of these values reverted to its previous state.

Midway through the course I was lying down after meditation when, in the most natural manner, I became aware that I was unbounded. Curiously, there is little more to say about it. Yes, I was unbounded. Yes, I did have a pervading sense of freedom because there were none of the usual boundaries around me, but all that seemed quite normal. It lasted, I would guess, only a matter of seconds. Still, the memory remains vivid. At other times in my life I had far more elaborate experiences that I'll go into at some point.

Have you ever had this feeling of unboundedness? The question conjures up the choice last words of Gertrude Stein. Lying on her deathbed, with her life partner in attendance, she suddenly sat up and said, "What is the answer?" When there was no reply, she asked, "In that case, what is the question?" Gertrude always had a way with words.

So did Voltaire, who also had friends in attendance as he awaited the end, reclining in bed. At one point a new arrival entered, causing the candle burning next to the bedside to flicker. "What," exclaimed the irrepressible dying man, "the flames already!"

Even better, to my mind, was his reply to a friend who said he had so many good spiritual ideas that he wondered if he should launch his own religion. "What would be the best way to start one?" he asked. To which Voltaire replied without hesitation, "The best way to start a new religion would be to get yourself crucified — and then come back from the dead!"

Death can be quite a lively subject. James Joyce wrote a fine short story called *The Dead*, and John Huston turned this poignant evocation of an Irish social rite into a film well worth seeing. Noted trial lawyer Clarence Darrow confessed, "I've never wanted to see anyone die but there are a few obituaries I have read with pleasure." And Henry James, with characteristic dignity, called death "the distinguished thing," and seemed to be looking forward to it.

2. Henry James' Siblings

Treasured Henry James! My guess is that if you asked prominent writers of today to choose their favorite English-language author, a good many would name Henry James, admiring his dedication to the craft of writing and his command of the medium, at once refined and complex, inspired and deeply caring. Much as I like him, I must admit I enjoyed William Faulkner's take. "James?" said Faulkner. "The nicest old lady I ever met."

Almost everyone knows that Henry had an equally renowned brother, William, the psychologist/philosopher who wrote *The Varieties of Religious Experience*, but few know there was also a sister, Alice, beloved of both brothers. Sensitive, intelligent, Alice could not match her illustrious siblings on their level and so she retreated, say literary psychologists, into recurrent invalidism, managing to find a sympathetic lady companion along the way and even writing a short memoir well regarded by critics.

Now hear ye! Were there yet more James siblings? Yes, indeed. Two more brothers, both younger and cherished equally by the elder contingent, but almost lost to history, this despite the fact that one was a Civil War hero who helped lead the first black regiment in that conflict, while the other tried and failed at various business ventures but was viewed by compatriots as one of the most engaging personalities of his time.

Of course we should not forget that young Gertrude Stein was once a student of William James at Johns Hopkins University, where she was planning a medical career that she early abandoned, leaving behind, however, a characteristic cameo. Called upon to write an exam paper, Gertrude left the page blank except for a note that said somehow she did not feel up to writing one at the moment. Her flexible professor let her know that he understood and did not penalize her. His patience, in future, would be more sorely tried by the Byzantine prose style of brother Henry, whom he frequently urged to be less opaque and more direct, admonitions that fell on deaf ears.

Despite their fondness for one another, William and Henry seem also to have coped with sibling rivalry. Whenever they were together, one or the other fell ill. Small wonder that sister Alice joined the indisposition parade.

The Jameses and Steins have diverted me for many an hour. Gertrude was of course the immovable force and brother Leo her intractable match. All went well in the early days of their Paris adventure in the budding 20th century. Leo knew a lot about modern art and guided their pioneering purchases of Picasso and Matisse.

But then Gertrude started to write, to write a great deal, and to view each word that poured forth as the near equivalent of Holy Scripture, not to be tampered with. For Leo, who had literary aspirations of his own, her voluminous output posed a growing threat. Moreover, to him it often seemed like jabberwocky. Reluctantly, he left the lair at 27 rue de Fleurus and the redoubtable Alice B. Toklas moved in.

When I myself lived in Paris in 1952 on a French Government Teaching Assistantship, Alice was still alive, though failing, and she might well have allowed me to come visit, lonely as she must have been after Gertrude's death in 1945. At the time I decided not to invade her privacy, probably just as well, since visits might have been taxing. Samuel Seward, an old friend who did call some years later and was received, reported that Alice's mind was clear but that her speech was severely impaired, causing her to linger laboriously over each word so that a short anecdote, worthy of only a few minutes, would drag on, and on, and on.

Which reminds me of my New York friend Edith Bel Geddes, who often interrupted people when they began the old cliché, "Well, to make a long story short." Just before they could say "short," Edith would interject "longer!" I met her while working at *Theatre Arts*

Magazine in the late 1950s when suddenly she burst on the scene as part of a new management team. Rather peremptory she was. I recall one day during a meeting she emptied some coins from her purse onto my desk and said, "Won't you get us some coffee?" I replied, "No, but I will ask someone to do so."

Since she was being difficult, I tried to think of something about her that I liked, anything to help break the ice. "You dress beautifully," I said the next time we met. That little remark did it. She looked at me from a different perspective and became much more sympathetic. Luckily I had been truthful in what I said. She often wore stylish creations by Chanel and Balenciaga and seemed to be to the manner born. Gradually we drew close and at least once a week for the next ten years she would invite me to dinner, sometimes with others, often alone.

Edith, I would wager, never seemed very young in her early years nor very old at later stages but always youthful, ever sweetly radiant, an adornment to any group she blessed with her presence. She had a large circle of friends because she was bright, vivacious, even mischievous at times, and a fine storyteller.

Many of the tales she told were about her three unusual husbands. Archie, her first, was a cousin who was really more than a handful. A spoiled upper-class adolescent when he married her, he amused himself, she told me, by firing pistol shots close to her feet because he loved to watch her agile moves as she dodged the bullets. Her second husband was a member of an old-line family that once ran the Boston Globe. After a session in bed he sometimes queried her in his New England brogue, "And do you feel the better for it, dear?"

Husband number three was the world-renowned stage and industrial designer Norman Bel Geddes who, she would recount, liked to lounge about in company in loose bermuda shorts that frequently allowed his male member to slide into view. This led her to devise a signal alerting him to the intruder. Often, however, he would be distracted by the conversation and miss it. When she repeated the routine he would become annoyed. "For God's sake, Edith, what is the matter?" he would demand. "You know!" she would firmly reply. "Why didn't you say so!" he would roar, whipping his wandering organ back under cover.

Before marrying this dynamic man, Edith was a noted costume designer, contributing to such top theater fare as *A Streetcar Named Desire* and *The Crucible*, as well as Jerome Robbins' popular ballet *Fancy Free*. She also helped produce Gian Carlo Menotti's opera *The Medium*.

Are you wondering how she was related to Barbara Bel Geddes, the popular actress who starred on Broadway and in the long-running TV show *Dallas?* She was her stepmother. Whereas Edith was chic, Barbara was understated, always pleasant to look at but simple in dress and manner. Though never close, the two respected and liked one another.

Over the years Edith and I took many carefree vacations together, most at her invitation since she had a wide range of friends around the globe. Amusing incidents abounded and I'll mention just one. A wealthy lady named Freda asked us to her hacienda in Mexico, a lavish facility with a legion of well-trained servants. Often we dined out of doors by a lovely little lagoon, sipping the local wine and chatting gaily. On this particular day we heard an unusual amount of levity emanating from the kitchen across the water.

"Why do you think they're laughing so much?" I asked Freda.

"They're probably peeing in our soup," she replied.

We all roared. After a bit, however, we became silent as we reflected on what she had said. Then we all remembered that her servants adored Freda and so we were in no danger. Our good spirits revived and we prepared our appetites for the meal to come. Minutes later, when the soup was served, we had a second guffaw even greater than the first. Can you guess why? Yes, believe it or not, the soup was split pea!

3. Garbo, Noel Coward, Marlene

While on the subject of *Theatre Arts* I want to single out one of our employees, a whimsical young girl named Ann, whom I hired to be a secretary. She did well and I rewarded her with a title on the masthead as "editorial assistant," a step that would look good on her resume. She liked the idea and relished her title, though her duties had not changed. One day, when our switchboard girl took a week off, I asked Ann to fill in and do little more than answer the phone.

To my amazement, she refused. "I'm an editorial assistant," she announced. "I can't answer the phone!" I said if she wouldn't do it I'd have to let her go. Even then she wouldn't budge. She left, this willful, eccentric, but interesting girl.

Oddly enough, we remained good friends. She went to work for the great conductor Leopold Stokowski. That, job, too, went awry. I asked her what happened. "Leopold wanted more than a secretary," she said. "He kept chasing me around the desk. Finally, I was getting more exercise than I could handle."

While speaking of Edith Bel Geddes I thought of Richard Burton, one of the many celebrities who came our way at *Theatre Arts*. Like Edith, he knew a great many of the noteworthy figures of our time. Of them all, he said, the two who impressed him most were Winston Churchill and Noel Coward, Churchill for the obvious reasons, the historical dimension along with his conversational verve, Coward for reasons similar to my liking for Edith — he found himself smiling whenever Coward entered a room, bringing joy in his wake.

Burton of course radiated star power and animal magnetism, usually directed toward the female gender. I witnessed it when he came to host a *Theatre Arts* awards ceremony. He was only of medium height, and his face was pockmarked, but he was attractive without a trace of narcissism. His eyes were at once friendly and flirtatious, and his stentorian voice a gift from on high.

Happily, Noel Coward also entered my life while I was working for *Theatre Arts*. When we ran a fine article about him and his upcoming Broadway musical, *Sail Away*, which was to star Elaine Stritch, we decided to put him on the magazine's cover and I called to see when we could take a photo. His assistant said they had lots of good ones already crowding their files, and so I walked over to the apartment on East 54th Street where the illustrious Noel lived. He himself came to the door and was the epitome of the word "dapper" as he showed me some excellent photos. When I gave them to our art director, however, he insisted on getting a fresh shot. This was then arranged to take place at Sardi's, where Noel and I met the next day for lunch.

I arrived to find him at a corner banquette with his secretary, female in this instance. The conversation was animated and at one point I said, "Elaine Stritch is such a great talent but she's somehow never enjoyed the stardom she deserves." "She will after this show," Noel said firmly. Only some hours later did I realize that the unpretentious "secretary" was really his show's leading lady and my remark therefore ill advised. What a gaffe! Still, on reflection, I don't think either Noel or Elaine caught on to my ignorance. If they had, surely their manner would have signaled my humiliation.

Some people, quite prominent celebrities, get away with a modicum of anonymity. About this same period, at the Brown Derby in Beverly Hills, I was having lunch with a correspondent of the Foreign Press Association. "Look at that woman," he said to me, indicating a buxom blonde passing by. "Can you name her?" I couldn't. "Ann-Margret," he said. It was indeed this lovely lady and no one was paying attention. The camera can obviously catch things the naked eye sometimes misses.

Here's another look at this phenomenon. Truman Capote tells of walking casually down New York's busy Fifth Avenue alongside

Marilyn Monroe, then in all her resplendent glory and with no one taking note of her presence. When he apprized her of it, she laughed. "Oh, you want me to be 'her?'" she said, drawing back her shoulders and assuming the Marilyn persona the public expected. Within minutes the street became her stage, with strolling pedestrians swarming in from all sides.

While interviewing people for my book about Greta Garbo, I heard similar stories about that unique star, who could appear almost dowdy in the harsh light of day but came to luminous life through the movie camera's lens.

One of the magic moments from her films occurs right at the beginning of *Ninotchka*, her first-rate comedy. Functionaries from the Soviet Embassy are at the railway terminal awaiting the arrival of their new bureau chief, expecting the usual drab communist bureaucrat. As the incoming passengers leave the train they search in vain for their man. Then the camera shows us someone's back and that someone turns around. Instead of the new male bureau chief, we see the startlingly beautiful Garbo. It's a great moment in films, though perhaps not quite as epic as the scene in *Gone with the Wind* where Scarlett O'Hara catches her first glimpse of Clark Gable, then at the height of his screen appeal.

During my New York heyday, roughly 1956 to 1968, I followed up my stint at *Theatre Arts* with another at *Show*, Huntington Hartford's performing arts magazine. After honing my writing skills, I turned to books, mostly Hollywood biographies — *The Child Stars*, *The Moguls*, *Garbo*, and *Sex Goddesses of the Silent Screen*.

Whenever I needed to see some hard-to-reach celebrity, I relied on two friends who had ready access to this world. Dan Blum, founding editor of pictorial annuals called *Theatre World* and *Screen World*, was one, and Edith Bel Geddes was the other. I was in my late twenties at this time, still a youth, but barely. Of course that last word reminds me of comedienne Joan Davis, who memorably said, "Ah, youth must have its fling — I wish someone would fling a youth at me!"

Edith sent me to Irene Selznick, first wife of the redoubtable David, who had produced *Gone with the Wind*. Surprisingly diminutive, though commanding in carriage and gesture, she received me in her New York suite at the Pierre, offering me a cocktail, which I accepted while she abstained. She told me of David's dealings with the other moguls and how he brought a young Alfred Hitchcock over from England to launch his Hollywood career. Later I interviewed Hitchcock at his bungalow on the Universal Studios lot. Surrounded by handsome Chippendale furniture, he sat with hands folded on his gently rounded belly and spoke in the same deliberate manner he used as host of his television series.

Edith also led me to Ruth Gordon, among many others. When I phoned, she responded in her inimitable drawl, much admired in *Harold and Maude* and other films. "I'm writing my own book, my friend," she said. "I'll be using all the good stuff. You wouldn't want me to give you any second-rate stuff, now wouldja?" The way it was said made it clear that even second-hand stuff was not going to come my way. Later, when I read her various memoirs and saw that she was perilously close to tapping third-rate material, I quite understood.

On the other hand, prolific screenwriter and biographer Adela Rogers St. John had no hesitation in running off story after story about Garbo and other Hollywood legends she had known over the years. I got the feeling she loved telling me about those bygone days.

The same holds true for William Haines, comedy star of numerous silent films and the most amusing, no-holds-barred person I interviewed over the years. For our session, he invited me to the West Hollywood home he shared with Jimmy Shields, his life partner. The house was modest but the grounds, on a quiet canyon, were extensive and the borders lined with somewhat weather-beaten classic statues that had once graced the estate of director George Cukor, who replaced them with newly cast originals. These I saw when I interviewed him a few days later. I also saw his guesthouse, where Katherine Hepburn and Spencer Tracy were long-term residents. Cukor, of course, directed the two in their highly successful series of films.

I'm digressing for a moment, but why not? If the aside is interesting, it's ok, right? Thank you. I knew you'd understand. You're a peach!

The first thing Cukor said when we met was this: "You're here to interview me. I'm not interested in your opinion of everything under the sun. Just remember that." What a beginning. "I will remember that," I said with complete sincerity. However, the moment we started talking I fell into old habits. When he expressed an opinion I shared I automatically began to echo it. I was going to say, "I completely agree," but remembered just in time. Instead, I said, "I completely...thank you for letting me come to talk to you." He saw what I had done and gave me a sly smile. "We'll get along just fine," he reassured me. And we did.

Coincidentally, I just saw a TV documentary on Cukor's career that told me something of which I was unaware. Apparently he was briefly involved with *The Wizard of Oz*, for which young Judy Garland had been fitted with a showy blond wig whose long strands of curly locks brought to mind a fairy tale princess. Cukor restored her to the more natural look that helped make her and the film such a success.

And now back to William Haines, who had been a top player in silent films and pretty openly gay, to the dismay of his employer, MGM co-founder Louis B. Mayer. When Haines failed to make it in talkies, Mayer may have been relieved. Haines went on to become a highly successful interior decorator.

At the beginning of our chat he complained that he was not feeling well. Several hours later he was rolling merrily along on his fabulous recall of the charmed years of early Hollywood. "I was sick when you came and this has made me well," he summed up. As a sample of his pungent delivery I'll cite a question I asked him about his old nemesis, Mayer. "Could you sum him up in one sentence?" I said. "What kind of man was he?" He paused for a deep breath and then ticked off, "He was a dyed-in-the-wool sonofabitch!"

During my interview sessions the star whose name came up most often was Garbo, and close behind, Marlene Dietrich. Edith Bel Geddes knew her quite well, was sometimes invited to Marlene's for dinner, and of course we all wanted to hear the details afterwards. "The food was delicious," she invariably reported. "The only thing I regret is that we hardly saw Marlene. First she was gone making a delicious meal, then she served it, and when we were done eating she disappeared again to clean up. I would have been happier if she'd ordered a deli take-out and stayed to chat with us. But she's wonderful. I love her." Who wouldn't? Who didn't?

When I was in the navy eons ago, I chanced to meet an officer who had been in charge of entertainment at various military hospitals during World War Two, which had just ended. During that conflict he had found it easy to enlist Hollywood stars for hospital visits, but when the war ended things changed. The patriotic fervor subsided and everyone seemed to have new priorities. The first Christmas after war's end he made call after call, only to find that every star he reached was engaged in some activity that made them unavailable.

Finally he thought of Marlene Dietrich, but hesitated because minor stars had turned him down and she was a major player. Nonetheless he dialed her number and she was called to the phone. When he hesitantly told her of his predicament, she swiftly said, "When do you want me?" She came, she saw and was seen, and conquered! He described her as tireless, going from room to private room to perform for bedridden patients after singing for the assembled group of those who were mobile.

4. My Sister and Jeanette MacDonald

As a young kid, one of the Hollywood stars who played a role in my life was Jeanette MacDonald, not only because my whole family loved her film musicals with Nelson Eddy, but because my Aunt Marietta bore a striking resemblance to her. Many years later I mentioned this to my sister Loretta. She startled me by saying that when we were young, and Marietta would be absent from the house from time to time for whatever reason, Loretta assumed that she was going off to her other life — as Jeanette MacDonald! What a delightful imagination!

Almost everyone in my family has similarly stunned me at one time or another. My brother Willard spent most of his life working as a janitor at the University of Iowa, an occupation he thoroughly enjoyed. Pushing a vacuum or some other cleaning instrument around by the hour left him free to think his own thoughts, he explained to me. The price for this freedom would seem high to many people but I applauded his attitude.

His own thoughts, which he seldom revealed to others, and to me only in our middle years, included several obsessions. When it came to snakes, especially pythons, he was ready to filibuster for an hour and every minute of it fascinating.

On the subject of German heavyweight boxer Max Schmeling, he could reel off each round of every fight Max had ever fought. Not only did Willard think often and deeply about this man he idolized, he also put pen to paper and wrote letters about him to boxing magazines. These were published and gained him a great reputation among Max Schmeling aficionados.

It never occurred to me until we spoke that there was an international network of Schmeling devotees who corresponded not only with boxing magazines but also with one another, exchanging memorabilia such as original letters and signed photographs. Willard was a major player in this network. He did in fact correspond with his idol over many years and Schmeling clearly enjoyed his end of it, reminiscing over his various bouts, analyzing the pros and cons.

He must have been a most genial man. Certainly in his native Germany, where he had a Coca Cola dealership that made him a second fortune after his boxing days ended, he was a great national hero, having taken on Joe Louis, America's best heavyweight boxer of the time, not only once but twice, winning the first, then losing the famous second fight which the charged atmosphere of the time turned into a battle between dictator Adolf Hitler and the democratic way of life represented by Louis.

Well, as if that weren't enough, Willard had a third obsession, and, who knows, maybe more, all conducted after hours of pushing vacuums and cleaning mops around at work. Cats. Willard was crazy about cats, any cats, but especially the 20-plus cats of Aunt Marietta, a.k.a. Jeanette MacDonald.

Why so many? Actually the number varied from month to month. Marietta was one of those people with the proverbial heart of gold. She could say no to no one. Living in a rather isolated house in a very tiny village, almost in the country, she started with a cat or two of her own, but these multiplied when farmers in the neighborhood saw that she was an easy touch and dumped their excess felines on her doorstep.

Willard's role in this cat carnival turned out to be that of historian, as I learned on walks with him. He knew every cat in that elaborate menagerie by name, usually bestowed by him, and not only their names but their interactions — which tom had savagely attacked which competing tom over which seductive female at what time of day or night. Listening to these accounts was mesmerizing.

Finally, of course, there were too many pussycats for the area, resulting in aggressive behavior and illness. A droll family member stopped by one day at the feeding hour and took a long look at the scruffy assembly. "So many cats!" he exclaimed. "And all of them ugly!"

Having tendered a quaint cameo in the life of my sister Loretta, and the more elaborate quiddities of my brother Willard, it's only fair to cite a few of my own.

Whenever I can I like to have motley colored rugs in my rooms because solid patterns, dark especially, pick up lint, and when I see little flecks on solid colors I feel compelled to remove them, no matter what other weighty matters need attention. Mamie Doud Eisenhower, first lady under "Ike," would sympathize, since she could not bear to see the nap of the White House rugs disturbed. When guests wandered through and left their glaring footprints it was standard procedure for the maids to vacuum the despoiled area and restore the nap. I could understand that perfectly.

Mamie was a native of Iowa — Boone, to be exact. Like the other states, Iowa has a good list of prominent native sons and daughters. Included, of course, are Herbert Hoover, Iowa's only president, and his first lady, Lou Henry Hoover, of Waterloo. Herbert was born in West Branch, a small town near Iowa City. So we've had one president but two first ladies, and also one vice president, Henry Wallace, for a term under Franklin Roosevelt.

Johnny Carson came from Iowa, born in the little town of Corning. John Wayne was born in Winterset, Iowa, as Marion Morrison. "Dear Abby," a.k.a. Abigail Van Buren, came from Iowa, as did Norman Borlaug, who made great advances in agriculture and copped a Nobel Prize for it. And James Van Alen, who discovered a radiation belt around the earth and was honored by having it named after him. And pioneer labor leader John L. Lewis, famed for his scowl and bushy eyebrows. And Harry Hopkins, considered one of the principal architects of Franklin Roosevelt's New Deal in the 1930s. One could go on and on with this quite thrilling list.

Well, all right then, I will. Peter Schickele, a.k.a. P.D.Q. Bach, hails from Ames, Iowa. And current Hollywood stars that started life in

Iowa include Tom Arnold, from Ottumwa, recent cinema Superman Brandon Routh, from Norwalk, and versatile Ashton Kutcher, from Homestead. Coincidentally, the star of the 1950s TV series, Adventures of Superman, George Reeves, was also an Iowan, from Woolstock.

Pollster pioneer George Gallup was born in Jefferson, Iowa. Artist Grant Wood first saw the light of day near Anamosa. And here's an oft overlooked Iowan, Robert Noyce, computer pioneer via Fairchild Semiconductor and Intel, born in Burlington, Iowa, and credited with developing silicon and so putting the silicon in California's Silicon Valley. The great bandleader Glenn Miller was from Clarinda, Iowa. Fashion maven Halston came into this world as Roy Fenwick in Des Moines.

Iowa has more than a thousand towns and cities, which include not only the just-named Jefferson, but also Washington and Monroe, and Paris and Rome. Of course nearby Indiana boasts of Peru, locally pronounced "pee-roo," the birthplace of Cole Porter — but Iowa makes up for that distinction by christening almost a dozen towns with the names of saints.

Which saints do Iowans revere and honor? Well, I thought you might ask. Here they are. St. Ansgar, St. Anthony, St. Benedict, St. Catherine, St. Charles, St. Donatus, St. Joseph, St. Lucas, St. Mary, St. Olaf, and St. Paul.

How about you, kiddo? Did you say Christopher, the saint who watches over travelers? A very nice choice, and somewhat predictable since you're definitely a frequent flyer. Oh, of course, you're wearing a St. Christopher medal. Neat.

Many saints come to my mind, but St. Theresa has a place on high all by herself. In addition to her other good qualities she had a robust sense of humor. I immediately think of a trip she took through some desolate region where everything went wrong until finally she threw up her hands and asked God why he treated her in this way. When God, to whom she spoke regularly, replied that this was how he sometimes dealt with his friends, she teased him, "No wonder you have so few of them." Just yesterday I read that she once said she had so much gratitude in her nature that even a small sardine was sufficient to bribe her.

Of course you know most of those Iowa town saints, except perhaps for St. Ansgar who was born of a noble family near Amiens, France, in 801, and became a monk at a monastery in Picardy. When the king of Denmark converted to Christianity, Ansgar went to Denmark as a missionary and so is known today as a patron saint of Scandinavia, which has sent many emigrants to Iowa.

Ansgar's sense of humor is undocumented but I like the remark made by a recent candidate for sainthood, the Catholic activist Dorothy Day. When told of this proposal to honor her she said sharply, "I would not like to be dismissed so easily." A lovely woman she was.

St. Francis had many virtues and was a frolicsome youngster, but once committed to monkish gear his humor did not often dominate. In Franco Zefirelli's fine film, *Brother Sun, Sister Moon*, however, there is a moment that drew a great laugh when I saw it. It occurred when St. Francis was meeting the Pope. To demonstrate the espousal of poverty by his monks he appeared in the nude. At one point the camera caught his shapely buns in all their saintly symmetry — and that incongruous view broke up the audience.

This reminds me of the great spiritual composer, Olivier Messiaen, who dealt only with the loftiest themes, causing the quick-witted composer and music critic Virgil Thomson to remark, "His aim is to open up the heavens — and bring down the house."

Virgil Thomson is one of those departed souls it would be fun to have over for dinner, if that option were open. If you could invite, say, five people to dinner at your house, whom would you resurrect? You yourself would be number six, of course.

5. My Debut in the Amana Colonies

From your raised eyebrows I bet you're wondering where I'm going with this unusual manner of spinning the various strands of a life. I'm certainly not favoring the sequential birth-education-career route, which has a tendency to be tedious, paying undue attention to dates. Instead, I'm using the device we all employ every day while getting to know people, moving freely from subject to subject, guided by memory and associations, with spontaneity the key motivator. These digestible portions of prose will add up in time to a fully drawn portrait, just you wait and see. It will be like nature's unfolding of a rose, petal by petal.

And now back to that proposed dinner party. Over the years I've plotted many a pleasantly ghoulish soirée of that order. One I would definitely enjoy would be comprised of: Gertrude Stein and her life partner, Alice B. Toklas; Ernest Hemingway, whom Gertrude liked initially but less with time, a chill that he repaid with a stinging glimpse of her household in *A Moveable Feast*; Scott Fitzgerald and his fabled wife, Zelda; plus myself to keep mayhem to a minimum.

I say that because, along with the Stein/Hemingway brouhaha, another might still be brewing. Zelda, almost on sight, was put off by Hemingway's macho stance and declared, "He's a phony," while he wasted no time in delivering his riposte, "She's crazy." He was no phony when it came to wine, so a good vintage would be required for this repast, and in plentiful supply. Maybe they'd all be so glad to see each other again that only fond memories would surface.

I have a plausible explanation, by the way, for Hemingway's insistence on his manliness. In his early teens he was very short, not much over five feet, and still short in his middle teens. Moreover, he had difficulty pronouncing a consonant or two, making him a possible figure of fun. And finally, his mother dressed him, for a time, in clothes that matched those of his sister of about the same age. So, sensitive to youthful taunts and perhaps jeers, he later pushed his macho image to the max. Happily for him, he made up for lost time by swiftly turning six feet tall. The rapid growth came at a price, however, leaving him less than fully coordinated and much prone to accidents.

Now, of the living, what sextet would you choose for a dinner party? The past offers a surplus of possibilities. The present supply, in my case, is so lean that I can quickly summon up what would very likely be the only current soirée I would care to have. My first guest would be winsome Dick Cavett, a master of repartee. To keep him company I'd call in Steve Martin, who is both versatile and amusing. I'd also invite Lily Tomlin, a great original and nobody's fool. And Bob Dylan, who is certainly a cultural icon of our time.

That splendid historian, David McCullough, would keep the conversation flowing, drawing on his vast knowledge of the pivotal figures he's written about, from Teddy Roosevelt to John Adams. We need one more guest, preferably another lady. Arianna Huffington gets my call. I read her well done books on Maria Callas and Picasso, and often enjoy her Huffington Post. Let's also ask everybody's current pet, Ellen DeGeneres. It will be a lively evening in my extended household.

The word brings to mind my birthplace, a large two-story red-brick dwelling with a cavernous, fully utilized basement, and an equally spacious attic filled with discarded household treasures — chairs and sofas of every variety, framed pictures of people and landscapes, a pioneer Victrola along with heaps of shellac records, clothing of that bygone era on hangers and in boxes, stacks of old newspapers and magazines, albums of family photographs. I still recall, in winter, the scampering of an attic mouse; in spring, the buzzing of myriad flies awakened from their slumber by sunshine streaming through the windows.

Did I tell you that the house had more than 20 rooms? Few bathrooms when I was very young, more and more as I grew older. No electricity at first, just oil-wick lamps and candles, but in the 1930s came electric lights and extensive plumbing. Was my family so large as to need 20 rooms? Let me explain.

The house was, and is, in a tiny town in southeast Iowa. You may have heard of the Amana Colonies, home of Amana Refrigeration, makers of Radaranges and other household appliances. The Amanas were a Utopian experiment — like the neighboring Amish community, and the nearby Mennonites — founded by immigrants mainly from Germany, who settled first in New York, near Buffalo, in the early 19th century, then went west when that city started encroaching on their unique culture. The trek to the heartland took place in the early 1860s. Looking down from a bluff, these pioneers recalled the beauteous plain of Amana in the *Song of Solomon*, and chose this site as their new home.

For economic wellbeing, members of the group pooled their resources and vowed to serve their community and God, having come to the New World to avoid political squabbles and wars on the Continent and to be free to worship as they pleased. The communal ways thrived for almost a century, stretching out over seven little villages separated by streams and forests. The men went into the fields to work while the women tended to household chores and the community kitchen.

Blacksmith shops kept horses in trim, although automobiles were crowding them out. Two doors from my family's home was a wonderful old general store, three stories of everything a household might need. I can still recall where the candy trays were, and many other displays. Each Saturday night the farmers would come in horse and buggy from the countryside and submit their names for a bushel basket of prizes. Their horses, tethered at a railing, would neigh, jangle their harness, and whip at the pesky flies with their tails. The following morning I would scour the grounds and sometimes find a nickel or a dime that someone had dropped. Oh, boy!

My entire family went to Sunday church services. Males sat on one side of the aisle, the youngest up front, with each succeeding row occupied by the next eldest group. Females sat opposite them in a similar progression, everyone on white pine benches. The wooden walls were without ornament. Church elders sat facing the congregation. The services were in German for many years and then eased onto bilingual German and English.

While I spoke both, living in the countryside limited my vocabulary. When the elders read passages from the Bible, the narrative registered but the meaning of their commentary often escaped me. One Sunday in particular, my brother and I grew very restless. For some reason, perhaps the gravelly tone of the elder's voice, we started giggling. If he had quickly finished his remarks, all would have been well. But he went on and on, the rasping delivery ever more pronounced. As a result, our mirth finally bubbled over, accentuated by hushes from the other elders.

Eventually the solitary voice subsided into silence and the service resumed. Willard and I knew, however, that trouble lay ahead. We fled as soon as church was out. We shared a false hope that we might find some safe spot to hide, and chose to nestle in the farthest corner of the barn that housed the village buggies. Dad and Grandpa, alas, read our minds, quickly found us, and were not too happy when they did. They knew we were basically good kids who had never been punished. Still, they made a game attempt to look stern. Each chose one of us, applied a mild thump to the rump, and told us this must never happen again. Hand in hand we all walked home.

I knew quite early on that our services were Protestant, a Pietist offspring of the Lutheran church, and that we had once had prophets who were in direct communion with God, with scribes taking down their every thought and revelation. At this early age I sometimes fantasized becoming a spiritual teacher, fleeting thoughts that adumbrated my later use of meditation as a tool for self-realization.

6. My Father Learns to Meditate

In the 1930s, again for economic reasons, the Amanas gave up their communal ways and turned capitalistic with a ready heart. Everyone was rewarded proportionate to the years of service. Some took cash while others banded together and received houses or small business ventures. The many branches of my family pooled their rewards and gained the hotel/restaurant set up as a transfer point between two railroads. I want to talk more about that serene rural atmosphere of long ago, but for now I want to give a glimpse of my immediate family.

So I'll start with my father. Good old Dad was a dreamer. He had a splendid baritone voice, which rang out on Sundays over the a capella choir in the church service. Singing with others came easily to him, but when asked to perform alone, in public venues, stage fright constricted his vocal chords.

He did, for a time, have a voice teacher from nearby Cedar Rapids, who set up a recital to be broadcast on the University of Iowa's radio station. I remember the tension in the air that day. Everyone in our house was as nervous as Dad, maybe more so. Conversation was minimal. And when in the evening the radio broadcast began, there was total silence. Dad was introduced and started to sing one of his best songs, "The Rose of Tralee."

Sadly, we all knew instantly that the old jinx was there. The voice sounded strained, drained of its rich mellow tones. In Iowa City, in the studio, Dad knew it, too, but was unable to overcome that dread invisible obstacle — fright of a stage that wasn't even there, an anonymous something that could not be conquered. He came home in a depressed state, which turned to anger directed at himself.

That depression remained to dominate his life. He simply didn't know how to cope with it, and no one was able to give him meaningful help. His days passed in dreary succession with routine work in the general store while he lived within his troubled mind. I saw him once in a childhood dream where he was caught in a tangled mass of prickly vines and brambles that held him tight while he struggled to get free.

Today I feel great sympathy for him. Then, it was another story. With his life a hopeless morass, he became negative and unpleasant. Every upbeat remark irked him, caused him to utter some damning rebuttal, often directed at my mother, whose side I took in their repetitive arguments. Their conflict, seldom about anything practical, found them at opposite ends of the philosophical spectrum. "Life is hell!" Dad would shout. Mom, quite cheerful by nature, would reply by bursting into joyous song that only compounded his misery.

There were moments when this predictable back-and-forth volley was almost humorous, like a well staged verbal tennis match. Sometimes I laughed, and sometimes I cried. Once, when I was perhaps six or seven, I lost control of my childish emotions because this time Mom was not up to the battle and clearly hurting. I ran between them, shouting to Dad, "If life is so terrible, why don't you end it?"

Fierce words, but neither of the combatants paid the slightest heed. So I took my case to God, imploring Him to do something. Since He was apparently busy at the time, I gave Him, too, a piece of my childish mind. All passion spent, I went out to play. It was a perfect sunny spring day, with a soft, sweet, healing breeze. I resumed being happy.

About 60 years later, after a lifetime of daily grousing, my father suddenly changed. He became mellow and tranquil, thoughtful and kind. Everyone noted the change, he most of all. One day I said to him, "You're a great guy now, a likable fellow, but do you have any idea how awful you used to be?" He looked me in the eye and calmly replied, "Yes." After a pause he spoke with firmness, his voice like the tolling of a bell. "Yes," he repeated, "and every single day I tried to make it better!"

The words tore at my heart. He knew! Through every tortuous day he saw what was happening and struggled to overcome his burden, to gain some control of his life and make it better for all of us. I felt a great love for him at that moment of revelation. I couldn't help but reflect on how little we know what's really going on in those around us. If we did, how much more understanding and accepting we would probably be.

I'm reminded of the time I was working with Anthony Quinn, the screen's great Zorba the Greek, on his autobiography. He told me about the man his mother married after his father died, a good man, he felt, but so unobtrusive that there seemed almost no one there, a life somehow wasted. But maybe not, it now occurs to me. Perhaps this inarticulate man had within him some revelations that would have astounded his stepson.

Are you wondering why my father's personality changed so dramatically late in life? Yes, maybe it was simply the mellowing of age. Or perhaps his astrological chart was in flux. Perhaps. But I think what happened was that he began to practice Transcendental Meditation. The technique provides a state of rest deeper than deep sleep, allowing long accumulated stresses to dissolve. That's what did it, I feel quite sure. Of course I may be somewhat prejudiced in favor of that theory for it was I who had already learned TM myself, swiftly become a teacher, and on this day crowned my career by initiating him. I must say that was a stunning event.

It happened to be a banner afternoon, fragrant with the scents of summer, cooled by a breeze caressing the leaves in the sturdy trees that shaded our house and those of us sitting on the porch, me and my dad. "What a beautiful day," I said, mostly to myself, but not quite. "Shit!" he shouted. "It's a shitty day, just like all the others!" This was vintage paterfamilias, so familiar to me that it hardly disturbed the tranquil moment. And so I replied with the same words I had used in this situation every time it came up since I had started meditating.

"Well, you can change all that," I would say, and said now. "It's so easy. Just start Transcendental Meditation. I can teach you." "No!" he would shout. And that was that. I had tried many times, same result always. Still I tried once more. "I can teach you right now," I said. "Your whole life will change. It's so easy."

I waited for the predictable reply. It didn't come, only silence, followed by the surprise of the year if not of a lifetime. "Well, if it's so damn easy," he said quietly, "why don't you teach me right now?"

My heart whirled into fast-forward. Dad had said yes, a word almost unknown in his vocabulary. For a man around 80, schooled in conservative modes of thinking and behavior, veteran of a lifetime of negativity, it was a startling reversal. I was able to rise to the occasion, thank heaven. For the brief ceremony that went with the teaching we needed some fresh fruit and flowers. There they were in the yard, flowerbeds and fruit trees aplenty.

An hour or so later, the entire quite momentous occasion was over. I had taught my negative father Transcendental Meditation. He was a bona fide beginner. He certainly looked more serene afterwards. So no doubt did I. What a weight off my shoulders! I knew in my heart the benefits that would now accrue. I felt so lucky that he had allowed it to happen, making me the instrument for putting him on the path to a better, happier, more enlightened life. That blissful summer afternoon is forever etched in my memory.

Henry James would understand. He once wrote that for him the most beautiful words in the English language were "summer afternoon." That day they also became mine.

7. My Mother in Close-Up

In the early stages of my writing career I asked a hundred prominent people to name the saddest word in the English language. Astonishingly, dozens of busy, gifted individuals took the time to reply. Editors told me this was most unusual. My request letters said I was working my way through college by writing short pieces for publication. Maybe that did it. In any event, the Reader's Digest published a good selection of the replies.

Here's a bunch I recall. Former president Harry Truman quoted John Greenleaf Whittier — "Of all sad words of tongue or pen, these are the saddest, 'It might have been.'" He apparently typed this out himself, and, having left out the word "of," inserted it by hand. Adlai Stevenson replied with the word "but." A week or so later, having forgotten that entry, he suggested the word "if." This neat tergiversation was vintage Adlai, it seemed to me. The Countess Alexandra Tolstoy, the great writer's daughter, contributed "war." So did labor leader Walter Reuther. Actress Katherine Cornell said "forlorn." Etiquette maven Emily Post submitted the word "regrets."

T.S. Eliot, no less, said, "The saddest word in the English language is obviously 'saddest.'" James Thurber, in large clearly legible handwriting — large because he was nearly blind — wrote, "Most writers start out like yourself by using other people's words as their own." Having lectured me on that score, he said that in his recent experience the actor Tom Ewell, in his Broadway hit, *The Seven-Year Itch*, made the words "sweetheart cherries" sound like the saddest words in the language.

Sad words and sad thoughts bring me back to Dad, who miraculously pulled his life out of its morass near the very end. There have been surveys that show that as the years go by we become more and more like the parent we like the least. That would make me a clone of Elmer Henry Zierold, a tough daddy early on, whom I grew to appreciate only in his later years. As I myself flirt with old age I increasingly note resemblances.

My father saw himself on the stage of the Metropolitan Opera although he could not pass muster at a local radio station. He was always fascinated by grandeur — by Versailles, the Pyramids, the Taj Mahal, the Grand Canyon, the Great Wall of China. He had no eye for workaday matters like driving a nail. He flunked cleaning up in the kitchen. He simply didn't register those things.

I'm much better at some of them, but I've never been known as the handy man around a house. Dad and I look alike, though he was always the more striking, a John Barrymore matinee idol in appearance. He gulped food down because it was not bringing him fame, so why waste a lot of time on it? I part with him on that score, considering food a spiritual entity. I do walk like my Dad, but then I think most sons do.

While I could go on about Dad, I feel Mom should have equal time at this stage. Just as he was handsome, she was very attractive. They looked wonderful together, as all the old family photos, which they both fancied, prove. On camera and off, my parents were "lookers."

Since they squabbled a lot, however, I often wondered what drew them together. They did produce children, and never once did I hear either of them question the wisdom of their union. So perhaps looks played a key role. Mom had rich dark brown hair, which came down to her shoulders at times. She was rather petite, moved gracefully, and had a gentle speaking voice.

I simply adored her as a child, in part because I felt so sorry for her, sorry because to my young mind she was stuck with my father and little love came her way, a view that changed as I came to realize their mutual accommodation. Mother was 29 by the time she and Dad married. When I asked my Aunt Henny why she had waited so long, Henny replied proudly, "No one was good enough for her!" Dad obviously was.

If I took a composite of how others viewed my mother, it would be hard to see how they could be describing the same person. A college friend once told me she struck him as a nice little German lady. True, she spoke German as her first language and on occasion sported the bonnets and shawls that were the custom in the community. She always wore white gloves on Sunday, when we went calling on relatives, feeling her hands were not attractive.

My novelist friend Marguerite Young once met her on a train, quite by accident, and thought she could have been a countess, so great was her dignified air. When I told Marguerite that she tended to run me down, she swiftly contradicted me, saying Mom had praised me effusively during their visit.

Of course, I think this may be typical. Parents praise their children to others, which redounds to their benefit, and treat them quite differently at home, where they assume the parental role as they see it, which means urging the children on to do better things rather than rest on their laurels. When I became a published author and sent her a little check to celebrate, Mom certainly thought it was wonderful. And more so when I appeared on the *Today Show*, interviewed by Barbara Walters, for a true-crime saga I had put into print.

But when, after seven or eight books, I tired of the grind and turned to other interests, becoming a teacher of Transcendental Meditation, the old censoring mother figure reappeared. Teaching TM was more a labor of love than of big bucks, she ascertained. One day, when I was in middle age, with a moderately successful literary track record but no great current income, she said encouragingly, "Norman, you'd make a good waiter. Why don't you get a nice job in a restaurant waiting tables?" Ah, mothers! Mind you, somewhere she may also be reminiscing and thinking, "Ah, children!"

Here's another view of Mom. While serving in the army during World War Two my brother Willard met a neat young German girl named Marion, later brought her to the US, and married her. Marion and Mom had what might best be called a guarded relationship. One day I said, "Marion, as someone who comes from outside the family, tell me, what kind of person is my mother in your view?" She laughed nervously, thought for a moment, and replied, "She's tricky." Well, people are kaleidoscopes. I think they are all those variant things that different people think they are. She was never tricky with me.

Dad was constantly tussling with Mom but if anyone else attacked her he came swiftly and forcefully to her defense. She did quite the same for him. One day I told her that for years Dad had neglected us when we were children. "What?" she said with controlled outrage. "Why, he would sit you on his lap and tell you stories by the hour!" It was true, and suddenly those hours came back to me, along with memories of how he would take us for long walks and tell us what animal tracks we were seeing in the snow and many other interesting facts. Underlying the tensions between Mom and Dad was a distinct respect, even admiration, and also some sorrow.

Perhaps the Greek legend of Diotima helps explain it. Once man and woman were united in one being, Diotima, but when that powerful entity threatened the Almighty, he split Diotima in two, creating man and woman, who were now condemned to search perpetually for their missing half. We come into the world alone and we make our exit alone. Johannes Brahms replaced his missing half to a degree with music, but is known to have said, "What is music without a little sadness in it?"

My mother could be very generous. She always ate sparingly, served her delicious meals first to others, shared any gifts that came her way, never went visiting without taking along some cookies or a loaf of home-baked bread. For a time she crocheted little thumb bonnets that she sold for a mere two dollars, though they took quite some time to finish. When I told her she could ask for more, she replied, "I'm satisfied with two."

But was she tricky, as Marion said? I guess she could be, but not in a mean way, more likely misguided. Once, when I left my literary endeavors in New York and came home for a visit, I did not alert the family to my arrival. As a result, passing by a downstairs window, I could see Mom and Dad seated in the living room, apparently engaged in pleasant conversation. Without their noticing I quietly entered the house by a rear door, climbed the stairs and washed, then came down refreshed and asked, "Mother dear, how are you?" To my amazement, she withdrew into a little huddled mass and replied in a small piping voice, "Not so good."

This sent Dad into upheaval. "Why, what do you mean?" he demanded. "Just a minute ago you were fine. You were laughing." From her quaint psychological retreat, Mom glared daggers at him, obviously ready to spit verbal bullets in both German and English.

When Dad, who tended to be gullible, tried to pursue the point, I interceded. "It doesn't matter," I said. "She'll be fine when we all go out to dinner — on me." I knew exactly what was happening. Mom wanted attention. She seemed to feel that if she feigned sickness, she'd get it.

For many years she had us worried because something was grinding away in her stomach. She brought this up so often that we were sure it was serious. We suspected cancer, of course, but the doctors said all was well. The situation took a toll on everyone around her but Mom survived and racked up a surprising 96 years before departing the planet.

8. Marvelous Marguerite Young

I'll go on about her after a detour limning my friend Marguerite Young, the novelist I spoke of a while ago and easily one of the most fabulous figures in my life. Promethean is the word for her. She was highly original, wildly stimulating, and excessive in many areas of life. She liked to sport colorful peasant-style blouses and skirts and these blended well with her open, gregarious manner.

I first met her in Iowa City when she was teaching there at the Writers Workshop but our friendship moved into high gear when we both moved to New York in the 1960s. As a young writer she had published two volumes of poetry and a well-received history of New Harmony, the 19th-century idealist community in Indiana. The monumental novel she was embarked on dwarfed these early efforts.

Miss Macintosh, My Darling, she called it, and it was known throughout the publishing world as a work-in-progress. It had been in progress so long, several decades, that by the 1960s it was legendary. Some questioned its very existence because of the lengthening years. Then one day, to considerable fanfare, Scribner took it to the printers and soon the reviews proved that it was a reality. The New York Times *Book Review* hailed it as one of the most significant novels of the quarter century.

During the final years of its gestation I chatted with Marguerite every day either at shared meals or on the phone. Her calls were beguiling and usually lengthy, often an hour or more — about the book, of course, with her reading new passages; and about politics, where she was of a potent liberal persuasion; and about friends, past and present. Sometimes, when the call went on longer than anticipated, I would put down the phone, go to the fridge and fix myself a snack. I would eat it in the kitchen and quietly return to the phone after my tuck-in. Though this happened many times, not once did Marguerite notice my absence.

She talked about Leo Lerman, the *Vanity Fair* editor, whom she liked a lot, and about fellow novelist Dawn Powell, whose writing she admired. She talked at length about Truman Capote, whom she had first met at Yaddo, the artist colony. She told me of a period when he would call her late at night from the apartment he shared with his mother, lamenting the difficulties he was having there. She spoke often about Anaïs Nin, whom she greatly enjoyed, though she felt her novels were too skeletal.

She introduced me to Anaïs, that ethereal looking but solidly grounded author of short novels and voluminous diaries. Anaïs invited me numerous times for lunch at the condo she shared with her husband at 3 Washington Square in Greenwich Village. I always found her in good humor, stimulating and gracious.

I was somewhat taken aback then when a mutual friend told me she had asked if I could be trusted. The circumstances were amusing. Anaïs had one husband in New York and another on the West Coast. She was apparently convinced that neither knew about the other, since she traveled back and forth without bringing the matter up with either.

Marguerite said it was the worst kept secret in the world. And now Anaïs wanted to know, or so I surmised, whether I could be counted on not to reveal this already public "secret." What she concluded, I do not know, but she did keep asking me to her welcome lunches. She also referred to me several times in her diaries.

Marguerite was dismayed when her monumental novel, though well received, did not make a bigger splash. She was consoled, however, by a vast cult following that kept in touch with her. On one occasion a New York radio station held a 24-hour reading of this massive work. When Marguerite died, a lengthy *New York Times* obit described her as "the Queen of Greenwich Village."

But earlier I vowed to return to the subject of my mother. For many years I wanted to write a short piece called, "The Most Embarrassing Moment of My Life," citing various celebrities. Mom was the key figure in my own such occurrence.

It was her birthday and because I knew she wanted a new teapot I went to a store in Marengo, a modest little hamlet only a few miles from Amana, to make the purchase. This was in the 1930s so remember the prices I cite are of that era. The store had only two teapots, one for $3.99 and one for $1.29. I was willing to spend $3.99 but the little $1.29 version looked better to me. I swear to God I thought it was the more attractive of the two! In any event, I bought it and gave it to Mom. I thought she would like it.

Alas, she did not. And how did I know? Because the next day she took it to the store, hoping to exchange it for another! There she learned that it was only worth $1.29 and that if she wanted the other teapot she would have to fork over the difference. She decided to keep the cheapie. Oh, what humiliation for me, to say nothing of her. When she told me what had happened I offered to buy her the more pricey pot, but she dismissed the thought. And here I am some 60 years later still protesting my innocence! That little pot was cute, I tell you. You believe me, don't you, dear? Hmmm.

Now, what is your own most embarrassing experience? I see you're blushing. You think that it would shock me, eh? Well, remember this, what shocks me would kill most people!

Sometime I may relate some of my early, bumbling experiences with girls, which, however, can best be described as pathetic rather than embarrassing. I'll skip them here except to confess that at the age of six I proposed marriage to winsome, brown-eyed Erna, who was perhaps five at the time, and laughed her little head off. Like Rodney Dangerfield in a later era, I couldn't get no respect!

I've always enjoyed the observations of a wise man when it comes to the sexual arena — "The pleasure is momentary, the position ludicrous, the expense damnable." True to a degree, but even overrated, 'taint bad, many would say, especially in youth. I always thought

George Bernard Shaw was the author of the saying, but apparently not. Lord Chesterfield is sometimes given credit but no verifiable attribution has been made.

In his lifetime, Shaw was so eminent that he was often referred to simply as GBS. Not many reach that eminence. Franklin Delano Roosevelt did, of course, with FDR. His predecessor, Herbert Hoover, never made it, and in fact a radio announcer of the time made a classic blooper, referring to him as Hoobert Heever. Nor did FDR's successor make the grade, since he had no middle name. True, he was sometimes called HST, but often with the caveat "Harry S-for-nothing Truman." Eisenhower didn't march to his initials either but won much of the nation's heart as smiling, folksy "Ike."

In putting together dinner parties of the departed, GBS is certainly one I would like to put on a list. He does present a problem, however. Though a great talker, he did not suffer fools gladly, and was not always the ideal listener. In his time, one could have invited him with Churchill, but Winnie likewise enjoyed holding forth and did not hide his annoyance when others took the floor. The scintillating Oscar Wilde, another marathon monologist, presents the same problem.

Perhaps one could add American-born Lady Astor to the groaning board. She was Winston's nemesis in and out of Parliament, and could hold her own with him. Wilde and Shaw, however, would not flourish if these two tangled. As moderator, perhaps I could give each guest equal time.

For the table of six, one more is needed, preferably a lady. Beauteous actress Lily Langtry would be just the one to ask. They all knew her, especially Wilde. Perhaps she would keep the conversation on a pleasantly frivolous level. Lady Astor might feel upstaged—but, dear heaven, one can't plan for every eventuality. Let her lump it!

In a similar vein, it might be challenging to have Garbo at a dinner party. When I was writing my biography of her in the late 1960s I interviewed quite a number of people who knew her either as friends or as co-workers on films, and for them it was never "Greta," but usually "Garbo" or perhaps "G.G."

How she did capture the imagination! My book was unauthorized so I never tried to interview her. She would refuse if asked, said the publisher, Stein & Day. I was warned that her friends might not cooperate but to my amazement many of them did. Nadea Loftus Dragonette, sister of popular songstress Jessica Dragonette, was especially helpful. She told me after the book came out that Garbo told her she liked it. So there was a feather in my cap. And McCall's ran a good section of it. Another feather, this one financial.

Much later, I was in the neighborhood of River House one day, on New York's East 52nd Street, where I knew Garbo resided. On impulse I stopped to chat with the doorman, telling him I had written a book about her and wondered if people still pursued her in her late 70s as they did in her heyday. A reserved Oriental gent, he became quite animated by my query. "Just this morning," he said, "she go out and come back running, with peoples running behind her. I quickly open door. Will never stop." Since Garbo made her last film in 1941, it had obviously not stopped over the ensuing decades, and probably continued apace until her death.

While I made no attempt to reach the elusive Swede, I did meet, over the years, any number of what the *New York Times* once called, in a column, Bold-Face Names, and curiously enough, the encounters were always unsolicited. It began for me in childhood, when I was perhaps five or six years old.

9. Navy Days and Mae West

As I've indicated, I grew up in a large house that was also a hotel/restaurant designed to accommodate passengers transferring from the Rock Island Railroad in Lower South Amana to the Milwaukee Railroad in Upper South, my home. People sometimes drove in via automobiles of the period but many came by train. Since I was always on hand, helping the ladies in the kitchen or running errands, I was given various assignments.

Initially, I was told to greet guests and escort them into the dining room until all the tables were occupied. Thereafter, I was to guide latecomers to chairs and benches on our front porch or on our spacious lawn, which was ablaze many months of the year with colorful flowerbeds created and watched over by elderly Aunt Emma, another denizen of our house.

While people were waiting, I often sat with them and made such conversation as was possible at my age, mostly responding to questions about the community and the hotel. One couple, training in from the Deep South for their annual stay of two or three weeks, took a particular liking to me, and planned their visits, believe it or not, to coincide with my birthday. On that occasion each year they presented me with a bushel basket of bounty, always including books. I devoured these and reported to them on the contents. Each year they grew more varied to accommodate my growth into adolescence.

After a time the visits ceased, but a correspondence ensued. I found myself writing to a Mr. Hudson Strode. Not until much later did I chance upon the name in the *New York Times*, which was reviewing a book by the man. Thus I learned that he was the author of a definitive multi-volume biography of Jefferson Davis, president of the Confederacy. He was also director of a well-known writers program at the University of Alabama.

Luminaries from the University of Iowa came regularly to our restaurant, where I met them without thinking twice that they held prominent positions, among them literature professors and the head basketball coach, who always came with his aged mother. All made friends with Aunt Emma, who was in the garden from sunrise to sunset, a lady with a green thumb if ever there was one.

In the same vein of innocent encounters, soon after my 18th birthday I enlisted in the navy and was sent to the Great Lakes Naval Training Station near Chicago. I became a storekeeper in the disbursing office, typing out checks for officers being released to civilian life. One day I recognized the name of Lieutenant Commander Harold Stassen, who in his political career was for a time governor of Minnesota and later ran eight times for president! Never a real contender, he persisted in order to air his points of view.

Lest I forget this, I enlisted on August 13, 1945, and the Japanese started to surrender the next day. Do you think there might have been a connection? You don't, eh? Rats! Back then to life at the Naval Training Station.

Often on weekends my navy buddies and I would go in to Chicago, which was considered the most hospitable of all cities to servicemen. We were lucky one evening at the United Service Organization, or USO, to get free tickets to a show called *Come on up, Ring Twice*, written by and starring Mae West. Its teasingly raunchy lines thoroughly pleased us.

Afterwards I lingered and savored the theatre, making my exit slowly when a voice called out, "Hey, sailor, would you like to meet Miss West?" I nodded and was ushered, along with others, into the star's dressing room. Almost immediately a rear door opened and Mae West undulated into our midst. She was tiny overall but curvaceously lush at the same time. Questions flowed, which she parried in her inimitable sensuous drawl. In the cast of the play a sailor had fared well after "coming up." I seized upon that recollection and said, "Miss West, I'd like to take lessons from the sailor in your show." She pursed her lips and smiled coquettishly. "You don't need to," she intoned. "None of you boys need to." A neat moment of light laughter followed.

Another free USO ticket came to me for none other than Jeanette MacDonald, whom my little sister years earlier believed to be in reality my Aunt Marietta. The ticket was not for one of her popular films with co-star Nelson Eddy but for a performance of Gounod's *Faust* at the Chicago Lyric Opera. Jeanette, an accomplished soprano, was singing the role of Marguerite, the female lead. My comrades and I loved it and went backstage afterward to her dressing room, which was already crowded with admirers.

In person, Jeanette, very lovely to look at, radiated star power and obviously knew it. I asked whether she and Nelson Eddy would ever make another film, a question which did not thrill her and which she skillfully navigated. Today I regret having posed it. How I wish that I had told her instead about my sister and her belief that our Aunt Marietta was, in fact, also Jeanette MacDonald in her spare time. "I'm really your nephew," I could have added. What a hearty laugh that would have induced!

Chicago's notoriously difficult critic, Claudia Cassidy of the *Chicago Tribune*, gave Jeanette's *Faust* a rave review, saying she sang beautifully, with "purity of line and tone." Cassidy even added humor to her praise, concluding, "You felt if Faust must sell his soul to the devil, at least this time he got his money's worth."

At this time it was thought that Nelson Eddy and Jeanette were often at loggerheads and not fond of one another off camera. Later it became clear that a strong and loving relationship existed for years between the two. Though various problems parted them, both continued to pursue successful careers, which in Jeanette's case included both films and opera.

When she eventually married actor Gene Raymond, these two became the central figures in one of the most amusing, risqué — and consequently oft told — tales of golden age Hollywood. Here's the basic plot as it was once relayed to me.

On this particular day Jeanette went away for the afternoon and was not expected back until evening. Gene invited a friend to come and play tennis at his court, battled him vigorously, so that by late afternoon both were exhausted and sweaty. Gene suggested that his friend might want to take a shower, an offer he readily accepted. Meanwhile, however, Jeanette came home early, and in a buoyant mood. Hearing the shower, she hurried to it, reached inside the curtain, and gaily exhorted the occupant, "Go get 'em, tiger!" The scene would fit neatly into a good French farce, n'est-ce pas?

10. New York and *Theatre Arts*

B ut back to the decades when I met so many prominent people, especially during my four years with *Theatre Arts*, a boisterous and satisfying rollercoaster. How amazing that I ever got there at all, since my Amana background was hardly a predictable prelude to Broadway! And yet, as an adolescent I had read library copies of *Theatre Arts Magazine* and entertained fantasies of one day working there.

Accordingly, when I decided that if I could make it there, I could make it anywhere, as the Kander-Ebb song goes, the first thing I did on arriving in New York in 1956, was to call *Theatre Arts* to ask for a job in editorial. I was told there were no openings there, nor in any other department, but the advertising manager did sometimes see people. I eagerly called the man in question, Ellis Meyers, who had been Hugh Hefner's adman early on at fast paced *Playboy* until a disagreement parted them. While Hefner went on to fame, even notoriety, and fortune, his advertising sidekick landed with more sedate *Theatre Arts*.

This nice man interviewed me, reiterated that there was no job now, but added that I should call once a month in case things changed. I did just that and each time the answer was the same — no change. At the 10th or 11th call Ellis told me no money was available to hire new staff. "Next month save your dime," he advised. I remembered this some 30 days later and decided to save that dime, then reconsidered and called once more.

"How soon can you get over here?" he said. Ten minutes later I was at 130 West 57th Street, where I began work as an advertising trainee at *Theatre Arts*, not quite my goal, but close enough. Under Ellis Meyers' excellent tutelage I quickly learned the ropes and had some success. A mere six months later the magazine changed ownership. The new people could not afford my boss's apparently substantial salary. He prepared to leave and recommended me to be his successor.

Thus, after less than a year in fabled Manhattan, I was the advertising manager of *Theatre Arts*, with a raise in salary, which led me to a neat studio apartment at 104 East 36th Street, in an area just below Grand Central Station called Murray Hill, named for a Mrs. Murray who entertained the British troops during one crucial afternoon of the Revolutionary War and thereby allowed American soldiers to slip away and fight another day.

After a pleasant lull at the office the new management asked me why more advertising revenue was not coming in. The current flow was steady but limited to trade ads from drama teachers and schools, lighting suppliers and the like. National advertisers were not drawn to our modest circulation of thirty-thousand subscribers, many of them in community theatres across the country.

"We can't get national advertisers because our circulation is too small", I explained, thinking quickly. "Why don't you take over circulation?" I was asked. We had no circulation manager as such, so that area was added to my portfolio. When some months later I was asked why our circulation was not growing, I again put my brain into fast forward and had a ready answer. "To gain new subscribers," said I, "the editorial needs to be much stronger, more punchy." "Will you give some attention to editorial?" I was asked. I acquiesced. At each stage of my ascent I requested a little raise — and got it.

My climb up the career ladder escalated when another top level turbulence shook *Theatre Arts*, with several claimants contending for power in an almost Marx Brothers atmosphere. I was told of a small dark valise that contained the company stock and of a chase between contending taxis racing down Fifth Avenue with this mysterious valise the prize.

In this rococo chapter, Peter Ryan, a dynamic and handsome Wall Street lawyer, announced he was the current chief of *Theatre Arts*.

Since he was busy with his law firm he asked me to be the editorial director and acting publisher of the magazine while he supervised my work during weekly breakfast meetings.

A heady and happy era of my life ensued, so engaging that the middle of the evening often found me still at work. Why leave the premises that fulfilled my adolescent dreams of a vocational Utopia! With gusto I scouted the current scene for candidates to make the magazine entertaining, informative, and relevant. I remember inviting Jean Kerr, the popular writer and wife of theatre critic Walter Kerr, to be our drama critic. She was pleased to be asked but said her husband, then with the *New York Herald Tribune*, was the critic in the family and that one, especially one with whom she so often agreed, was enough.

When a friend told me that an up-and-coming young man designing print ads for I. Miller Shoes would make a fine art director, I called up — Andy Warhol! We had quite a long chat. The modest monthly stipend I was offering did not deter him. He listened carefully to what else was involved, debated, and came to a decision. "I don't want to lock myself in to design 32 pages of theatre copy every month," he concluded. Oh, the astute fellow. He always knew what he wanted.

In each issue of *Theatre Arts* we ran the complete text of a play. Since we had a film issue once a year someone suggested that we use it to run a film script, specifically Charlie Chaplin's *Monsieur Verdoux*, which had never been published. I immediately called international information for Chaplin's phone number in Vevey, Switzerland, where I knew he, his wife Oona, and their children resided. I was given a number, called, and asked for Mr. Chaplin. "This is Mr. Chaplin," came the surprising reply. He, too, listened, said he would consider the matter, and be in touch if interested. Clearly, he was not, and this time the modest fee was perhaps a factor.

So far I've given only instances of editorial initiatives that led nowhere but I've done so to show we were really active in every area. The results led to a well-received editorial content and a breakthrough in national advertising.

Finding a strong drama critic was fun. It was my good luck to hear about Alan Pryce-Jones, a former editor of the *Times Literary Supplement* in London. When I called him, he invited me to dinner to get acquainted and the restaurant he chose was the fashionable Café Nicholson. I had a good time with this debonair man-about-town and he reviewed plays at *Theatre Arts* for a year or so until his boss at the Ford Foundation, where he was fully employed, ordered him to stop moonlighting with us.

On request, Alan recommended as his replacement the man covering theatre for the scholarly *Hudson Review*, John Simon by name. I approached John and he accepted our offer. He was at once brilliant, erudite, and often witty, with strong opinions and a presence that quickly won him a following. After a time, I asked if he'd like to do some media interviews, promoting both himself and *Theatre Arts*. When he agreed, I placed numerous calls on his behalf with good results. He once credited me with launching him in this area.

While highlighting the stage, *Theatre Arts* also ran an opera issue each year, and this led me to call on Gian Carlo Menotti, then at the height of his fame, the composer of *The Medium*, *The Telephone*, and *Amahl and the Night Visitors*. What I remember most is that on rather short acquaintance he offered me a job as his secretary. It might not pay a lot, he explained, but it would give me access to anyone I wanted to know on the current scene, opening the door to a career of my choice. Since I was already meeting many cultural icons, I let his invitation pass.

The years at *Theatre Arts*, certainly one of the most satisfying periods of my life, came to an end when the magazine again changed hands, around 1962, and the new owners put their own team into place, leaving me to forage elsewhere. Yes, indeed, I missed the bracing daily routine, the gratis theatre tickets, and gourmet dishes at prestigious Voisin, along with lively moments at Sardi's. Both restaurants ran ads in *Theatre Arts* in exchange for meals.

I landed with *Show, the Magazine of the Performing Arts*, where I became circulation director, working for Huntington Hartford, an heir to the A&P grocery chain fortune. Anyone employed by him had to pass a graphology test, which he personally supervised. I forget what the sentence was that he used, but I wrote it, he inspected it, and I passed muster and was hired. About a year later, alas, the magazine was abandoned and my pleasant tenure came to an end. Hartford also owned Paradise Island in the Caribbean, along with a jewel-box museum on New York's Columbus Circle. His numerous ventures failed, passed into other hands, and in many cases came to fruition under new ownership, due in part simply to more favorable times. After leaving his employ I took the plunge I had long contemplated and began my writing career.

11. Poulenc and Classical Composers

I'll soon get into the writing game, but while speaking of Gian Carlo Menotti I thought of some other musicians I encountered over the years, among them the versatile composer/author Ned Rorem, definitely a people person. When we met in New York we chatted and learned that we had both lived in Paris for some time in the 1950s, yet had never met there. No matter, since I learned about his years in France from his revelatory Paris and New York diaries. Today he is acclaimed for his art songs, operas, and lyrical chamber works, which I find most rewarding. The composition that gave him the greatest pleasure throughout his life, however, was not by himself but by a Frenchman.

If you guessed Erik Satie, you'd be right, but I bet you'll never think of the work's title. I listen to music a lot and have never heard it played on FM radio. No, it wasn't the *Gymnopedies*. Try once more. *Three Pieces in the Shape of a Pear*? No, but you made a good guess, since Satie was engagingly eccentric in his titles and his life overall. At his death they went to his room in the Paris suburbs and found twelve identical suits in the closet. This was really odd because he seldom wore suits.

As for the work Ned Rorem revered, it's called *Socrate* — or *Death of Socrates*. Based on texts by Plato, the 30-minute piece was composed for orchestra and four sopranos. Satie said he wanted it to be "white and pure like antiquity," and claimed that he ate only white food while composing it. Sometime, my dear friend, we will have to listen to it together.

In New York I also ran into avant-garde composer Edgar Varese at a Greenwich Village cocktail party, but just after we were introduced, and launched on a promising conversation, he was swept away by two voluble ladies who monopolized him completely thereafter, and so I remember nothing said by eminent Edgar Varese. Some encounters with figures of renown do fizz out. Quite the contrary was the case with the greatly gifted composer Francis Poulenc. I'll explain how I came to meet him.

After my naval service I became eligible for the GI Bill of Rights benefits and applied to Harvard, Yale and the University of Chicago. All three accepted me but when there were delays in the other two, I opted for Harvard, which was quicker on the trigger. On graduating in 1949, I applied for a Rhodes Scholarship, was a finalist, but not picked. I was then recommended for a Fulbright Scholarship. Again, I was still being considered near the end but not accepted. However, I was recommended for a French Government Teaching Assistantship. Once more I applied and this time I was a winner.

How lucky I was! For the Rhodes I would have studied political science for several years, a tedious prospect in hindsight. Instead, Fate pushed me into a marvelous sojourn in France. This illustrates what a success seminar I once attended emphasized — When one door closes, don't despair, for another will open and bring you even better fortune.

Soon after arriving in Paris I sent a letter to Francis Poulenc at the instigation of a friend who had written a short piece about an elephant and thought it would be perfect for him to set to music. Quite promptly I received a reply to my letter, brief, friendly, from the Hotel Beau Rivage in Lausanne, Switzerland. He would be returning shortly to Paris, Poulenc wrote, and gave me a number to call. I complied. He himself answered and within minutes I was on my way to his apartment overlooking the Luxembourg Gardens.

Poulenc was tall, with an imposing oval face of great character. He moved with elegant ease. I recall much rich brocade in his cheerful living area. I sat down in a sumptuous chaise, foolishly offered my host a Pall Mall cigarette, thinking that he might appreciate this American weed. Clearly he did not. "Bonbon?" he offered in turn from a ready dish. I declined. He then suggested that I sit on the sofa nearer him. Again I declined, saying I was comfortable where I was. In retrospect, I'm amazed he didn't throw me out at this point. My youth made him forgive me, perhaps. And I was presentable, "sortable," as the French put it, neat and fresh and not bad looking, thanks to my family genes.

After 10 or 15 minutes of banter he told me he could not put my friend's elephant story to music because he had just done so with a story about a donkey — or perhaps it was the other way around. In any event, the answer was in the negative. I prepared to leave, but he said no, I should stay — and why didn't I come and sit nearby on the sofa. I still felt fine where I was and did not move, when the phone rang.

It was someone close to him calling and I could easily make out that he was learning that a friend of his had died. I believe it was another composer. With many exclamations of regret the phone call ended and we returned to our chat, with me again volunteering my departure. "Non, non," he repeated, when the phone rang again.

Within seconds it was clear that another ami had bit the French dust. Again he uttered exclamations of regret. I gathered that this time it might have been someone from the world of ballet who had departed permanently. Again, when the phone call ended, I offered to leave, becoming increasingly eager to do so, but no, no, I was told, not when we were just getting started, and why didn't I come and sit…

Then, unbelievably, the phone rang yet once more, and once again an almost vaudeville-like repeat began. But this time, when I arose, my deflated host escorted me to the door. I should call him again, he said quietly as I returned his wave and left.

When I met him in Paris, Poulenc was close to the half-century mark, maybe just beyond. At nineteen, in reply to a music publisher's query, he had written, "I do not like Beethoven at all. I loathe Wagner. The four influences on my music were Bach, Mozart, Satie, and Stravinsky." How amazing that this musical genius should have known himself so well at this early age — and how fortunate, for it must have spared him many an experimental misstep. While I hardly knew his music when I met him, I have grown to love it for its exuberance, gayety, and inventiveness, and also, at times, for heartfelt spirituality.

It took me five or six decades to refine my tastes in music, and today, at four-score years, I have some views that only lately surfaced. I recently shocked a friend and music-lover by saying it would cause me no regret if I never heard Beethoven's nine symphonies again, not ever, not in this lifetime. My friend gave me a startled look and spoke somberly, "Please move away from me so that when lightning strikes you I shall be spared."

Mind you, I did not say that I disliked Beethoven, as Poulenc had done. I love many of his works, but having heard certain ones countless times I would rather listen to something new and different. I do, however, understand Poulenc. Great as Beethoven is, there is often a Teutonic heaviness there, the antithesis of Poulenc's inherent French vivacity. Ditto Wagner, though he is also a musical genius.

Poulenc loved Igor Stravinsky, who avoided listening to Wagner all his life and made some catchy critiques of his oeuvre, comparing the leitmotifs to a telephone directory. Late in life, however, his friend Robert Craft daringly took him to Carnegie Hall for an orchestral concert of Wagner. Midway through, noting the silence emanating from his companion, Craft looked over anxiously — and saw tears streaming down Stravinsky's face. "Magnificent," said the latter. "Magnificent." Very likely Igor had avoided Wagner for so many years because he feared his powerful influence might dominate his own work.

Do you remember what that never failing wit, Mark Twain, said about Wagner? "Wagner's music," he said, "is better than it sounds." To think that if we had been around in the time of Mark Twain we could easily have met him. In his later years, a Manhattan resident, he lived on lower Fifth Avenue and each day about noon, dressed all in his usual white and sporting a great mane of white hair, he would stroll up the avenue to the Plaza Hotel, where he would sit in the lobby and chat with friends and admirers. He was born, by the way, in 1835, the year of Halley's Comet, and often forecast that he would leave when that comet came again. Indeed, right on schedule, Halley's reappeared in 1910 and Twain died in the same year.

My friend Jim Thompson and I were comparing notes on music one day when I told him of my Beethoven heresy, which I extended to several other composers. He rather wisely asked me if there were some classics I had heard countless times and still wished to rehear, like perhaps Debussy's *Clair de Lune?* He had me there. If it's well played, I always love that enchanting work.

I could say the same for Debussy's *Afternoon of a Faun,* and, yes, Beethoven's sublime *Archduke Trio.* I have certainly never tired of Schubert's effervescent *Trout Quintet,* which I'm told is the most popular piece in the entire chamber music repertoire. The Samuel Barber *Adagio* from his string quartet holds a secure place in my heart, as does the *Adagietto* from Mahler's *Fifth Symphony.* I hasten to add the hauntingly beautiful *Bailero* from the *Songs of the Auvergne,* compiled and scored by one Joseph Canteloube, who actually heard two lovers use this serenade to communicate—at the incredible distance of four miles—across a mountain valley in this little-known region of France.

Do you find there are some classics you would readily part with for the duration of your years on earth? Are there others whose appeal is unflagging? Remember, these questions become more pertinent with age. When you're under 50, surfeit may not yet have set in.

I'm reminded of a concert I attended a while back at Carnegie Hall. I was a guest in a comfortable box seat. A grande dame in the adjoining niche turned to me after we had heard the first of Bach's *Brandenburg Concertos.* "One down, five to go!" she boomed. While I could now forego all six, fine as they are, there are other Bach pieces that I never tire of, including those spirited piano concertos as played by Glenn Gould. I'll probably always welcome the slow movement from Mozart's 21st piano concerto, often called the *Elvira Madigan* because it was the recurrent theme of that lovely Swedish film. I'll put it in a separate category. I've heard it very often, and might not choose to play it myself, but if I turned on the radio and there it was, well, I would not be able to turn it off. I simply could not. I just couldn't do it, I tell you!

To reward you for your patience in letting me air my musical tastes, let me relate two anecdotes that will amuse you. Opera composer Giacomo Puccini was a close friend of conductor Arturo Toscanini. Each Christmas, Puccini sent all his friends a delicious cake. One year, however, the two old friends quarreled after Puccini's cake was already on its way. Hurriedly he sent a telegram to the maestro saying, "Cake sent by mistake!" By return telegram Toscanini replied, "Cake eaten by mistake!"

Gioachino Rossini was not only a great opera composer but also a man of unfailing good humor. One day he was out walking with a friend, gaily discussing pleasantries, when they ran into a fellow composer, who asked Rossini the customary, "How are you?" Rossini sighed and said, "Not at all well, not at all well, but thank you for asking." After offering lengthy condolences the man went on his way. Rossini's friend thereupon expressed his surprise at the encounter. "When we were talking just moments ago you seemed very cheerful," he said. "Yes, I know," replied Rossini, "but it makes my colleague so happy to think I'm having problems that I said what I did to please him."

It seems that whether we like it or not, some people enjoy the sorrows and difficulties of others. The Germans have even coined a word for this phenomenon — "Schadenfreude," which is often translated as "satisfaction or pleasure at someone else's misfortune." Some cynical pundit has declared, "To be truly happy you need not only a good success for yourself but also a friend with a big failure." Ever apt La Rochefoucauld opined, "We all have the strength to endure the misfortunes of others."

12. A Long Snowy Drive to St. Louis

On that note, it might be a good time to see how you're doing with this memoir of a life in flux. My aim, as I've said, is to make it unreel in an easy, spontaneous manner. By now you've picked up the main threads, my worldly bent and my spiritual drive. Which will prevail? Only reading on will tell!

If we were conversing in person there might be days when one of us felt irritable, or overexcited, or inattentive. A graceful exit from a meeting might be a problem. No such thing worries you with what you have in hand. One of the best things about a book is that when you've had enough of it you can clap it shut and go about your business. "There is no frigate like a book to take us lands away," wrote Emily Dickinson, "nor any courser like a page of prancing poetry."

I know you read books but do you also sometimes reread them? Gore Vidal tells of reading and rereading Michel Montaigne all his life. I must say that admirable as Montaigne is, I would not be able to duplicate that feat. Noel Coward said he had painstakingly persevered through all six volumes of Marcel Proust's masterpiece, *Remembrance of Things Past*, but that he would never, ever, go at it again. It seems this resolve was firmed up by a passage where Proust took three pages to get a character from the top of the stairs to the bottom.

I've often marveled at how fecund Mother Nature is, giving time and energy to produce gifted individuals like Montaigne, Proust, and Noel Coward, then throwing away the mold, as it were. All three are unique, and while they and others on earth share certain characteristics, no two are completely alike. All eight billion current inhabitants of our planet have a different fingerprint! So, the unique aspect and the shared qualities coexist.

Repetition is certainly a staple of nature. Without its myriad seeds the dandelion might not survive. Most plants have a remarkably fertile reproduction mechanism, which gardeners admire in flowers but tend to deplore in weeds. Each year I find looking at nature more exhilarating, the wonder of it all, how the entire apple tree comes out of the empty space in a seed, from the nothingness, from what is absolute rather than relative.

And the human brain, with its hundred billion cells, is becoming ever more fascinating to scientists and laymen alike. And so are the heavens, where we are told that the earth is part of a galaxy that is only one of many millions — or is it billions? Doesn't it just boggle the mind? And in each galaxy there are billions of suns — or is it trillions? Boggles galore in either case!

Could this fantastic extravaganza have popped into being all by itself, spontaneously, without a creator? Could it have "just happened?" I love the story of 19th-century atheist Robert Ingersoll and his visit, with a friend, to the Metropolitan Museum of Art in New York. Coming upon a ravishing still life, Ingersoll exclaimed, "Exquisite! Who did that?" To which his friend wittily replied, "Oh, it just happened!"

In music, it seems to me repetition can be a pleasure, but within limits. And these limits, to me, are often transgressed in music by the symphony and sonata form where there may be many variations on a modest theme that is hardly worth even a first hello. I applaud Debussy, who cast traditional forms aside and traced his own enchanting musical language. Like many avant-garde composers, he felt constrained by the past, but just going for novelty without a core of beauty is hardly a step forward. It was marvelous Mozart who said, "No matter what music is expressing, it should be beautiful." Hear! Hear!

As I've indicated, it amuses me to see how composers regard one another. "Warily" is probably the best way to put it. Wagner liked the music of only a few contemporaries, among them Franz Liszt, whose daughter Cosima he had married. Surely that alone could not have swayed the great man! What? You think it might well have? Hmmm. He also admired the compelling innovations of Hector Berlioz.

Except when talking about himself—which was certainly a good deal of the time—Wagner could be quite comical. When one day someone brought up Schubert's *Trout Quintet*, he asked, "What next, *The Herring?*"

Brahms, too, was capable of a good quip. In later years especially he could be testy and vent his spleen on party guests. On one occasion he spared almost no one—and became aware of it just as he left. "If there is anyone here tonight whom I have not offended," he declared, "I beg his pardon."

As a young man, Brahms once brought a manuscript to Franz Liszt, who was always ready with his time and counsel and played it through, praising it highly. After hearing several other works of young composers, he played one he himself was working on. At its close his eyes swept over the assembly until he came to Brahms — who had fallen fast asleep. Liszt got up, went to his room, and purportedly never played a composition by Brahms at his public concerts, though when they met he was ever amiable. Brahms later blamed his failed manners on travel fatigue.

Brahms and Tchaikovsky had mixed feelings about one another's music but on occasion enjoyed each other's company—though Tchaikovsky did jocularly describe his symphonic colleague as "a big-bellied boozer."

While there was a good deal of sniping among composers, there was also much admiration and praise. Bach admired Vivaldi and transcribed more than a score of his works. Beethoven said he would always bow at the feet of Handel. Mozart admired Haydn and Haydn told Mozart's father that his son was the greatest composer alive. Bela Bartok greatly admired Liszt, asserting that he may have spawned even more musical innovation than Wagner—quite amazing praise.

Music brings back thoughts of my father and a touching incident in his blighted singing career. The time was the Great Depression in the early 1930s. Orchestra leader Paul Whiteman was very promi-nent on the musical scene at the time and my parents learned he was coming to St. Louis for an engagement. This, my parents decided, was their big opportunity. They would go to St. Louis, meet the great man, and Dad would ask him for an audition.

Naïve perhaps, but miracles are not unusual in show business. With high hopes, Mom and Dad, dressed in their Sunday best, got into their Model A Ford and set out for the big city in distant Mis-souri. Mind you, the season was winter and in the Midwest of that long-ago era winters could be very severe. This one was. A snow-storm developed en route and driving became more hazardous with each mile. Gallantly they persevered, guiding the little car through the drifting snow. After a strenuous and harrowing day they made it to St. Louis in the middle of the evening.

Having learned where Whiteman was staying, they arrived at his hotel and were told he had been delayed by the storm but was still expected. They sat in the grand lobby and watched the hotel traffic come and go, newcomers shaking the snow from their coats, head-ing for the hotel restaurants, which my parents knew they could not afford. So they waited — and waited.

And then the miracle came closer. My Dad's keen eye spotted Whiteman, surrounded by an entourage, heading for the elevators. Hurriedly he made his way over through the crowd just as the eleva-tor arrived.

"Mr. Whiteman, I'm a singer," he blurted out. "Can I have an audition?"

Impatiently, Whiteman took a quick look and spoke even more hurriedly. "Not on a night like this!" he said in staccato tones, stepped into the elevator, and was gone.

And poor darling Mom and Dad, weary and dismayed by this abrupt brush-off, came to a quick decision. There was no miracle in store for them. They could certainly not spend the money to stay the night, and so they made their way back to the Model A and began the long dispiriting trip home. The snowfall had abated and afterwards they recalled how silent the night and the journey had been.

One has to remember that they had a very limited use even of the English language, let alone the complicated ways of the larger world. Back home in their small sequestered village they often wondered what they could have done, what they should have done, what they might have said, replaying each stage of the drama. But eventually one fact was clear — it was over. A door had closed on my father's career.

I've heard it said that we choose our parents. Usually, when I broach this possibility, people brush it aside, saying they'd never have chosen individuals they've found to be so difficult. But presumably our choices are guided by the desire to have the fastest possible evolution. When we make the decision to choose our next family we know that the ensuing life may entail difficulties but also that the end result will be beneficial. It all makes sense to me. On first glance my parents and I seem to have had precious little in common to draw us together. So why were we entwined if not to work out some things that forced us to grow.

Robert Frost wrote a fascinating poem on this subject called *Trial by Existence*. It tells of a great meeting where a bunch of former Earth people, now on a different plane, are apparently getting ready for rebirth. They are given a number of choices for their next life, told the pros and cons, and left to make a decision. Mind you, that's how I view the poem.

What a marvelous poet Frost was — *Birches, Mending Fence, After Apple Picking, Two Tramps in Mud Time, One Acquainted With the Night,* and so many more wonderful works. In recent decades he has had a rough time, largely due to biographer Lawrence Thompson, whom he anointed for the job early on, only to watch him turn against him. Unwilling to withdraw his word, Frost allowed Thompson to remain, resulting in a psychology-driven biography that seems to me most unjust. Fortunately, more objective and favorable critiques are coming into print.

I would have enjoyed meeting Frost. In his later years he taught a good deal in college venues and would often allow a student to walk him home, and then, unwilling to face the night alone, he would turn about and walk the student to his dorm. When that was done, the whole amusing procedure was repeated. Frost loved company, though he did most of the talking. When asked to give a reading, he always ascertained if other poets would be asked. "Either I'm the show, or I don't go," he would candidly explain. His ready humor comes through in his suggested epitaph: "Lord, forgive my little joke on Thee, and I'll forgive Thy great big one on me!"

In his early years Frost often praised Emily Dickinson, but she received less attention from him as time went on. My guess is that as he grew in his own abilities he wanted no distraction, especially not from so powerful a peer as Emily. How I adore her, how I vibrate to her verse. So much so, in fact, that at times I wonder if I might be Emily reborn. She died in 1886 and I arrived in 1927, the year Lindbergh soloed across the Atlantic, so I or she would have had time for a nice rest between lives.

13. Thoughts on Enlightenment

D o you believe in reincarnation? It certainly makes sense to me and greatly enriches the present. When Maharishi Mahesh Yogi was asked the question, he said he was against reincarnation. What he meant was that he wanted everyone to become enlightened in this lifetime. Once enlightened, the soul merges with the absolute, he said, and so there is no need to come back, the goal already attained.

Would you like to be a saint? An enlightened person is in essence a saint, it seems to me. To become enlightened one has to release all stress from the nervous system and so gain full use of one's physical and mental potential. Well, that's quite a hefty order. A frictionless nervous system is in complete harmony with the laws of nature and makes no mistakes. All action is spontaneously beneficial for one-self and the environment. Life is bliss. A saintly state, wouldn't you agree? What's not to like!

Many people have glimpses, usually brief, of this hallowed realm. William Wordsworth, in *Ode on Intimations of Immortality* and else-where, poignantly describes transcendental moments he had in early years and how they later ceased — "The things that I have seen, I now can see no more." The purity of the childhood nervous system facilitates these glimpses, it has been conjectured, but the pressures of adulthood gradually erode them.

Tennyson tells of repeating his own name, using it as a mantra to induce transcendental awareness — again, moments only, which later fell off. Richard Bucke, in his book *Cosmic Consciousness,* takes a trip through the past and quotes other writers and philosophers who accessed the transcendent, giving special emphasis to his friend, Walt Whitman.

I've often wondered how Walt would have fared if he had used his given name, Walter. *Leaves of Grass,* by Walter Whitman, somehow does not strike the proper chord. Yet, Walter Winchell did well with his full first name, as did Walter Cronkite.

The great modern dance pioneer, Isadora Duncan, said that over the years she had many experiences of celestial light — often a concomitant of higher states of consciousness — but could not sustain them. Her nervous system, she surmised, was not strong enough to withstand their intensity.

Speaking of storied Isadora brings to mind another, more recent, modern dance luminary — Martha Graham — whom I encountered several times. One minute and I'll get to her, but first a concluding word on transcendence and how to sustain or increase that experience.

Meditation that gradually infuses the transcendental state into the other states of consciousness — waking, sleeping, and dreaming — can be a boon. Having learned the Transcendental Meditation technique almost 40 years ago, I can testify to its efficacy in this pursuit of Nirvana. I'm not all there yet by any means but I feel I've certainly made progress. So have over six million people worldwide who were taught TM and happily furnished subjects for some six hundred scientific studies confirming its wide-ranging benefits. TM is certainly the most widely researched self-realization technique of our time, and probably of any other.

I must relate an amusing situation from my earliest days of meditation. The experience is different for everyone who learns, of course, depending on the state of the individual nervous system, but for a bunch of us who began at the same time the key element gradually became euphoria. I recall writing and telling all my friends of this great discovery, so keen was I to spread the word. Along with feeling good came a desire to change aspects of my behavior to make them more positive, more harmonious.

This mood also overtook a young friend of mine named Alicia, who examined every aspect of her life, gave up this and that as being wanting in one way or another, and finally vowed to go one step further — she would make amends for irregularities in her past as well.

One thing the dear girl recalled was a long ago incident with a mail-order book club. It seems she had sent them a check for some books, apparently made a mistake in the amount, and overpaid by several dollars. She swiftly received a refund, in which the book club made a mistake of its own, sending her a sum that was too large by several dollars in her favor. At the time, she debated briefly with herself, then decided she did not want to waste any more time on the matter. She cashed the check and forgot about it.

Now, however, embarked on her new path of swift evolution, she determined to rectify this somewhat shady, though trivial, transaction of decades past. She wrote the club's treasurer, explained her situation, and offered to make amends. There was no reply to her missive. This was not surprising, since she could recall neither the date nor the amounts in question.

She was not one to give up this chance for salvation so easily, however. She expanded her correspondence to include other executives at the book club, pleading her case. The only reply said her request had been sent to the appropriate department and she would hear. Eventually a note arrived saying there was no way to trace her long-ago transaction and therefore no outstanding debt.

This was only a red flag for Alicia, spurring her on to a spirited telephone campaign. I overheard her trying to cajole a poor secretary into finding someone to accept her check. "I want to send you money I owe you! Money, money! I must send you money!" she insisted, all to no avail. In desperation she asked the secretary if she could mail the check to her as a personal gift. Thus, while the sum — now firmed up at four hefty dollars! — would not go to the company, at least it would reach a company employee, thereby assuaging her guilt. The secretary, flustered by the unusual conversation, nixed this magnanimous offer and shortly Alicia found herself haranguing a dead line!

Finally she gave up. Her friends, informed at each stage of her penitential crusade, were convulsed with laughter by these accounts of her plight. Years later, when I ran into Alicia at a party, we both recalled our enthusiasm during those first months of meditation.

I've always been in awe of artists and writers who slip into the transcendent. Imagine Mozart conceiving in one great flash the whole of a majestic opera like *Don Giovanni*. Or Schubert, riding in the Vienna woods and asking that the carriage be stopped so that he could write down the melodies he heard floating in the air for everyone to hear — only he alone heard them. Actually, Brahms heard them, too, when he was in the Austrian Alps writing his violin concerto. The air was so full of them, he told friends, that one had to be careful where one walked for fear of stepping on them!

No, I haven't forgotten Martha Graham, that peerless performer and gallant woman. When I lived in New York in the 1960s we had the same physician, Dr. Amos Cobert. Amos was a friend as well as a physician to his patients — who also included Eleanor Roosevelt — so much so that he often engaged in personal chitchat with them while half a dozen people were waiting to see him. That's how I first encountered Martha, who did not seem in the least impatient. She began telling me how in her early years she would go to the Central Park Zoo, just off Fifth Avenue, and study the movements of the animals, planning all the while to make use of their gestures in her choreography. Unthinkingly she would imitate the zoo dwellers — until people started watching her instead of the animals, at which point she would move on.

There was a period in her life when she became largely paralyzed. Through Amos Cobert she regained full use of her limbs and good health overall. Small wonder that she did not mind waiting to receive his ministrations.

I saw her several times in his office and then once more, a few years later in Fire Island Pines, that lush and lovely summer resort for the Manhattan art and literary world. She was seated on the deck of Peggy Fears' restaurant/bar, watching the yachts move lazily in and out of the harbor. She was wearing a broad-brimmed hat to shield her from the summer sun and a skirt and blouse that the artist Mondrian would have admired. We saw each other after I sat down, not too close and not too far away, for I didn't want to intrude on what looked like her reverie. We were the only people on the deck. The late afternoon was sweet and serene, bathed in silence.

After about an hour I did look over again, and this time she spoke. "It pays to be patient, doesn't it?" she said quietly. "It certainly does," I replied with a light laugh. And we both left it at that.

14. Tantalizing Trivia and Memories

What quaint little turns the mind will take. Cobert seems like a French name. The moment that thought came, the word "guillotine" followed. Why? Because I had just read that in France today it's illegal for media to show that dreaded instrument. Many people know that it was another doctor, Joseph Guillotin, who invented it. Probably not quite so many realize that he intended it as a more humane form of legally taking a life and was greatly dismayed by its role in the French Revolution.

Sometimes friends and I try to come up with people who have given their names to things. Do you know about "maverick"? More than a century ago a Western stockman named Maverick would not follow suit when his fellow ranchers branded their cattle. Consequently, unbranded cattle came to be called mavericks.

Everyone knows that England's Earl of Sandwich conceived the culinary treat named for him. Also well known is the Peche Melba — half a sunny peach filled with vanilla ice cream and topped with raspberry sauce — named for Australian opera diva Nellie Melba. I'm getting hungry.

Here are a few anomalies. French fries may first have seen the light of day in Belgium. Scotland Yard is in England. And of course Polish jokes are told principally in America.

Getting back to French fries, there's good evidence that in 1853 Commodore Cornelius Vanderbilt was at the Moon Lake Lodge in Saratoga Springs, New York, having difficulty with his order. The fries were too thick, he kept repeating as he sent them back. Finally, the chef made them thin enough to please this demanding guest. Thus, potato chips were born.

And that brings to mind another set of variants. Probably the best-known queen of France, Marie Antoinette, was Austrian. Catherine the Great of Russia was German. Certainly one of the best-known male rulers of France was Napoleon Bonaparte, who was born in Italian-speaking Corsica and always retained an Italian accent. The current English monarchy was spawned in? Yes, that's right — Germany.

But let's return to people who gave their names to things. The Chesterfield overcoat or greatcoat, replete with velvet collar, was first worn and popularized by a 19th century Earl of Chesterfield. A flush toilet or privy is sometimes called a "crapper," and credit for its invention is often given to Sir Thomas Crapper, whose company marketed authentic style "sanitary ware" until closing shop in 1966.

Sir Thomas held nine plumbing related patents, but the first flush-type patent was issued to British subject Albert Giblin in 1898. The association with Sir Thomas's last name seems to emanate from World War I when American doughboys in England saw the Thomas Crapper name on toilets and took to calling them "crappers." "Crap," furthermore, does not necessarily derive from "crapper," say the specialists I just consulted via Google. It could come from Dutch "krappe," or German "krape," a vile and inedible fish. In the popular mind, however, "crap" from "Crapper" seems the best fit.

And while on the subject — not crap, that is, but objects named for individuals — let's not forget French trapeze artist Jules Leotard, who gave his name to the clinging one-piece garment still worn today by ballet dancers and acrobats.

Well, one oddity category leads to another, doesn't it? For years I've been collecting unusual word derivations. For me, leading the list is "pumpernickel." We know it as a sourdough bread using unbolted rye flour for the dark variety and rye and wheat for a lighter version. Now then, we must skip back to the era of Napoleon Bonaparte and his disastrous invasion of Russia, where bit by bit everything went wrong. Long before the final retreat, the French soldiers complained of the hard dark Russian bread. Disdainfully they called it "pain pour Nicole." Nicole, mind you, was Napoleon's horse at the time, so they were calling it bread fit for a horse to eat. Over time, "pain pour Nicole" evolved into "pumpernickel. As you yourself repeat it, you'll see how that happened.

Still in a French vein, the word "dandelion" comes from that noble language, meaning "dent," or tooth, of the "lion." Look at the tooth-shaped yellow petals and it makes sense. Now just today I read that when the Moors came to Spain a millennium ago they saw rabbits jumping about everywhere. Because the Moorish word for rabbit is "span," they called the land "Hispania." Can you guess what the dogs that chased the rabbits were called? That's right — spaniels.

All these bits of tantalizing trivia have not made me forget the subject of saints that I broached some time ago, remember? Happily, I think we may have had at least one budding saint in the family, my great-aunt Emma who lived a life of service for others — family, community, and God — always cooking for others and gardening in the huge yard surrounding our house. Those were the days when people still had lots of flowerbeds of myriad shapes and sizes. Later, when hand lawnmowers gave way to motor mowers, the modern desire for speed made flowers retreat to the borders of the lawn.

I can still see Aunt Emma standing in the bright summer sunlight, a white cotton bonnet shielding her head, shears in hand as she trimmed a prolific pink rosebush that flourished all summer long. She was rather round-faced, her graying brown hair usually tied in a bun. She spoke very little, usually only in response to others, and while her English was limited, she could make herself understood.

A treasured family anecdote comes to mind. Guests who came to know her in her gardening mode often asked to see her later during dinner. She hated these interruptions to her kitchen duties but felt she must be hospitable. Rather than converse over a hot stove, she would invite them to her room for a small glass of Amana wine. One evening this familiar sequence was unfolding when Aunt Emma, leading her glowing guests toward her room, suddenly turned back to us and said in German, "Ach Gott, wass ein Elend!" — "O God, what a pain!" It was not easy for us to stifle our laughter.

A superb cook of soups and sauces, she always waited for a spare moment to take a dish of food for herself. A rest after the evening meal was often followed by her descent into the spacious cool basement, where there were great heaps of potatoes which lasted all winter long, bushels and bushels of apples, wrapped individually in old newspapers so those that spoiled would not affect others, and many jars of canned fruits and vegetables. There were also great vats of sauerkraut and other delicacies that needed care from time to time. One of my best youthful memories is of going down for apples and hearing Aunt Emma singing her favorite hymns as she worked.

Curiously, Aunt Emma, Aunt Marietta, and my mother all had foot problems, slowing them down. This sometimes worked to the advantage of the children in the house. Once a week, in the evening, we would wait till everyone had left the kitchen, bide our time, and steal back to make ourselves a batch of fudge, which we knew we shouldn't do. The only person likely to detect us was Aunt Emma, but her slow walk gave us time to hide all traces of our illegal activity. What fun that mischief was, and what tasty fudge! I'm getting hungry again.

Aunt Emma was a lifelong celibate, but because my paternal grandmother was at the time in delicate health, the family decided that her little daughter Marietta, my Aunt Marietta. should live with her and make her two rooms her own. Marietta, a well-behaved and pretty child, was completely happy with this turn of events and adored her surrogate mother. She shared much of Aunt Emma's days and slept in the huge double bed with her at night.

This occasioned another family anecdote. When Marietta grew up and married, she felt so tied to Aunt Emma that on her wedding night she could not bear the thought of leaving her suddenly by herself. Quietly she slipped out of her bridal bed and tiptoed downstairs to her old quarters. Silently she found her usual place in the great double bed and soon fell asleep in that familiar den of repose. Upstairs, her new husband slept...hmmm, fitfully.

In addition to rich soups that required hours of preparation, Aunt Emma specialized in apple fritters that she herself would sometimes carry to the dining room, much to the delight of guests, who would engage her in conversation, however halting. Only one subject aroused her ire — politics, of which she understood nothing at all.

One of our relatives was an elected official, a Republican Party representative in the state legislature, where he was numbered among the most virulent anti-Roosevelt faction. When he came to visit Aunt Emma, most of his time was spent savoring the tasty dishes she offered him, but inevitably he would lash out at the latest villainies perpetrated by President Franklin Roosevelt. Guileless Aunt Emma eventually succumbed to these diatribes against the Democratic "devil." Since many of the restaurant guests were Democrats, they got quite a shock when she would innocently ask them, "What we will do with that wicked man in Washington?" No one ever took offense. Whatever she said was a thing of wonder to her fervent admirers, who saw that she was merely being loyal to a family member and completely, and comically, out of her depth.

The family Republican, I should add, was also a country doctor, residing in the nearby small town of Williamsburg. He was considerably overweight, helped in his obesity by these snacks with Aunt Emma, and always late on his rounds. It was said of him that usually the baby was born ere he got there. When he was asked to run for lieutenant governor one year he declined, feeling he was not yet ready.

The man who was ready and did run, Bourbe Hickenlooper, was elected in a Republican year of victory, while the good doctor, having missed that running tide, never regained his place in politics. I recall his coming in one day after the news spread that FDR had died. "Well," he said slowly, taking a quick breath after each syllable, "the S.O.B. finally committed suicide." The current political scene in America may look savage to some but for me it's just par for the course. While each major party had partisans in our dwelling, we all wisely left the topic of politics alone.

What a wonderful thing it was, especially for the young and the elderly, to grow up in a house where so many branches of the family resided under one roof. The senior members always knew they'd be taken care of in times of poor health. I well remember how everyone took turns sitting with my father's parents and with Aunt Emma when each in turn became ill and their lives slowly ebbed away. It was all so easy and simple and loving. Doors in the house were never locked. When, of an evening, one branch of the family was indisposed, we kids would skip blithely down the hall to visit another wing. Eventually we'd wind up in our family rooms where by now all would be quiet, prompting us to have a fine pillow fight before sinking into deep childhood sleep.

Besides Mom and Dad, Marietta and her husband, Adolph, usually called A.T., and Aunt Emma, the household also included my paternal grandparents. Actually, all three of the children of these grandparents lived in the house — my father, Elmer, his younger sister, Marietta, and an elder sister named Helen Turner. Helen had left the community as a young woman to go to Chicago and be with her husband. When the marriage did not work out, she returned home to Amana with her two children, sweet youngsters named Bill and Doris. There they were down the hall of the great sprawling house, ready playmates when needed.

A couple of years ago, when my sister Loretta and I had one of our many reunions, we got around as usual to reminiscing and I was astonished to hear her describe our family as "dysfunctional." What? Our family, my family, dysfunctional? It was true, of course, that Mom and Dad bickered quite a bit. And yes, Mom and Dad took a dim view of Marietta and A.T., who reciprocated that wariness in spades. But what the heck! Didn't every family have something or other? That's what Mom said one day when I broached the subject to her.

For most of the time that Mom and Dad were at logger-heads — through the first 50 years of their marriage, that is — Mom was more or less at peace. She enjoyed the many simple pleasures of life and they compensated for much of the daily combat. I think the spats kept her alert, enlivening her whole physiology. While Marietta and A.T. also had their clashes, they were far less serious. "If we don't have a good fight once a week, I know something's wrong," Marietta told me one day.

Curiously enough, Mom and Marietta had several points in common. Both would erupt in sudden laughter, especially over human foibles. Both were compassionate and honored the tradition of family closeness.

I remember when we learned that crooner Bing Crosby had died, Mom became very thoughtful and said softly, "Ach, der Arme." "Ah, the poor fellow." Once, at someone's birthday party, Marietta noticed a neighbor lady gobbling down treats at a quite alarming rate. "Ah, the poor thing," she said sympathetically.

However, I seldom heard Marietta, who really liked almost everyone, speak kindly of Mother, except once when she conceded that in her prime Mom was a hard worker. On the other hand, when one day I said to Mom that Marietta was always thinking of others, she jumped right in with, "And never of herself," which was a neat insight and a sweet concession.

15. Emersons, Bernhardt, and Lincolns

When considering relationships, what a relief it is to know that everything that happens to us was somehow engendered by ourselves! All my life I've heard the old maxim, "As you sow, so shall you reap." It never fully registered with me until I had been meditating for quite a number of years and then only because Maharishi made it one of his most oft-repeated themes.

Not that it's easy to live with this maxim. When someone says something disagreeable, or acts in a thoughtless way, we have a tendency to reply in kind, launching an argument from which very little good can ensue. If we could just stop, reflect, and say to ourselves that we, rather than others, hatched the negativity, it would be much easier to handle. Of course we may argue that we have always been nice to the offender. Maharishi would reply that this was perhaps not true in a previous birth, where we may have hurt the person. So we have to accept reincarnation for this theory of action to apply.

For me, no difficulty arises. Apparently we can reap right now what we sowed long ago and the rascal currently causing us trouble is only a messenger delivering our due, our karma. The lovely thing about this insight is that it saves our psychology. No need for a knee-jerk response.

Mind you, it's not always easy to act in such a civilized manner. This knowledge may be of no help when the circumstance is so sharp that you simply have to say, "Go to blazes!" to the offender. Perhaps even that will be too mild and some choice expletives will be required. Better forgive yourself if you have such a relapse and promise to do better next time.

Here's an anecdote that also may help when someone is, say, giving you a hard time. On a morning stroll, the Master tells his disciple always to look for the good in people, for the brighter side of a situation, no matter how dire. Just then they pass the rotting carcass of a dead dog already prey to flies, wasps, and maggots. The smell, too, is unpleasant, and the disciple says, "Master, I see no good aspect to this dreadful sight." The Master smiles and replies, "Have you noticed the dead dog's shiny white teeth?" So, always look for the upbeat note in the dilemma at hand, perhaps the one good quality in an otherwise odious individual. Remember, what you give your attention to will grow in life.

Speaking of expletives, the other night I was listening—on National Public Radio, no less—to a group of highly reputed jazz musicians as they bombarded the airwaves with a wretched word that kept repeating like a tom-tom. The offending word was "motherf—r," and by its use the musicians meant nothing at all negative, in fact, often quite the contrary, as, for example, when one speaker said, "That motherf—r came in and showed the rest of us what jazz was all about."

But let's get back to the more uplifting subject of enlightenment. To help gain it, Maharishi counsels close attention to various facets of life, such as food, which should be nourishing and wherever available organic; a daily routine that gives the system sufficient rest; and an environment supportive of our high goal.

Money helps. I've heard him laugh when someone brought up this point of finance. "Of course, money can be a help to evolution," he said. "With it you can get a better guru!" He's always ready with a quip, even when discussing the loftiest subjects.

Invariably, he is surrounded by flowers, which he often plays with during his talks. On one occasion, when the subject of reincarnation came up, he gaily waved about a carnation and laughingly proclaimed, "One carnation is enough."

Over a period of more than 30 years I have never heard him cop out on a question. Often his replies are somewhat startling. Once he was asked, "What should we do if we read a negative article on the Transcendental Meditation movement?" "We should rejoice," he replied, drawing quizzical looks. "Ours is a positive movement," he continued. "Anyone who writes about us will have to say some nice things, some positive things. Those who are interested in us will hear the good and dismiss the negative. So we should rejoice."

Rejoicing is probably his most central theme. Since the ultimate nature of reality is bliss, he says encouragingly, we should become its embodiment. On one occasion he was sending out teams of meditators to countries that were in perilous turmoil. To those who volunteered to go he cautioned, "Don't go if you are not happy. What we have to offer the world is happiness. If you don't have it within yourself you cannot give it to others." He often quotes a preeminent passage from the Upanishads: "From bliss all beings are born; by bliss they are sustained; and to bliss they return."

"The individual is cosmic," he likes to say. "Man is not meant to suffer."

Another favorite saying is, "Do less and accomplish more." For this, of course, he provides the technique of Transcendental Meditation, which means closing the eyes and letting the mind employ a mantra, or sound, to go effortlessly inwards to the source of all energy, intelligence, and happiness — the transcendent.

Emerson comes to mind, and with him his remarkable Aunt Mary Moody Emerson, a tiny, birdlike dynamo who greatly influenced him. "Go for the highest!" was her lifelong creed. Philosophic but eccentric, too, was Mary Moody, in the best New England tradition. Approaching a ripe old age, and as always eager to be prepared, she knitted herself a funeral shroud. Then, however, she lived on and on. Why waste the shroud, she thought, and began using it as a shawl around the house. Still her body showed no signs of wearing out and soon the neighbors sighted her on her daily horseback ride with the funeral shroud wrapped about her tiny frame and flapping in the breeze.

Of course celebrated French actress Sarah Bernhardt later went her one better. Preparing for her own demise, she purchased a coffin.

On testing it she found it rather comfortable and converted it into a bed. Photos of "The Divine Sarah" artfully posed in her coffin delighted her legion of admirers.

Interestingly, Bernhardt was once on a transatlantic liner that was undergoing great turbulence when she saw an elderly lady on a staircase about to lose her balance. She quickly came to her rescue and found that she had performed this service for Mary Todd Lincoln, the bereaved widow of Abraham Lincoln, who was seeking solace abroad after his assassination.

Did you know that Honest Abe's eldest son, Robert, figured in no less than three presidential assassinations? Still only a young Harvard student, he was home for a holiday and invited to attend Ford's Theatre on that fateful night in 1865 when John Wilkes Booth shot his father. Tired from his journey, he demurred. All his life Robert regretted his refusal of that invitation, convinced that he might have prevented the assassination. In 1881, Robert Todd Lincoln became President James Garfield's Secretary of War and was present some six months later when Garfield was shot in a train depot in Washington, D.C. by a disappointed office seeker. Finally, in September 1901 he was on the train platform in Buffalo with William McKinley when an assassin shot that ill-fated chief executive, who died eight days later.

Here's a final and amazing Booth connection with the Lincoln family, again involving a rail terminal. This time, in the early years of the Civil War, Robert was on the platform of a rail station in Jersey City, en route home to Washington. As a train approached, the waiting crowd pushed him toward the tracks. He lost his footing completely and began falling into the abyss between the platform and the oncoming train when a strong hand grabbed his collar and pulled him to safety. In gratitude he gazed at his rescuer and recognized the well-known face of the great Shakespearean actor, Edwin Booth, older brother of John Wilkes Booth!

16. Maharishi in Close-Up

But what little white lie was I telling you when we got off on this macabre track? Was it perhaps something about my love life? Now what could have reminded me of that? Well, just about anything. In my early years, the first 45 or so years of my long adolescence, I pretty much succumbed to the Playboy philosophy. I would say 99 percent of my waking thoughts were about the chase, though in my naïve youth it often masqueraded as romance, or as looking for love, or whatever.

Romance, love, fiddlesticks, say I. It was glands, the overexcited glands that motivated most of my waking hours. I was chasing and being chased, and seldom the twain did meet. As a friend of mine once remarked, "When someone likes you, you're not interested; when you like someone, they're not interested. Here's a howdy-do." This was amusingly put, and at least partly true.

On the other hand, when I was working at a glamorous job in New York, residing just off Park Avenue, and definitely living the high life, I asked another friend, who happened to be a Catholic priest, why my studio apartment had only a small narrow bed rather than something queen- or king-sized. He instantly replied, "Norman, you're a monk at heart."

For the moment, I'm in a far better state than during those years of perpetual excitation. Now, instead of mulling over carnal matters most of the time, I hardly think of them at all. I eschew them. I'm quite fond of that word. How about you? I beg your pardon. Did I hear you correctly? You eschew it? You eschew "eschew?" Bless you! You win that round, clever one. Anyhow, my life is not as rousing this way, but more satisfying on a deep level. Why go for an animal existence when something more substantial, more rewarding, is at hand?

Well, yes, for me that is Transcendental Meditation and the world vision it has brought me. Still, in all fairness, in order to give a complete picture, I cannot totally put it down, that turbulent youth of mine. It's just that I now know you never "get away with" anything in life. If you indulge too heavily in any physical pursuit, there may be a price to pay somewhere along the line.

I'm quite aware that feeling regret or guilt is a waste of time. Recently I read that well into her 90s the remarkably durable Kitty Carlisle Hart was still performing nightly shows at Michael Feinstein's cabaret at the Regency in New York. In an interview she related that she looked at herself in the mirror each morning and said, "Kitty, I forgive you for everything you did in the past." The burden of guilt was just too heavy to carry around, she concluded, and wisely so.

That all made sense to me. And of course she could counter negativity with great memories of her career in show business, her happy married life with theatre genius Moss Hart, topped by her later, admirable, public relations stint for New York City. But can one really dismiss guilt or regret as easily as all that? In my case, when moments from the past come up where I failed some person, or hurt someone, however involuntarily, an unstoppable wave of regret sweeps over me.

As I've indicated, my father lived much of his long life with a profound sense of frustration and failure, his dreams of a singing career unrealized. I tried to console him late in life. "Look at it this way, " I said. "Even if you had been a big success, if you had sung at the Met, or had a great concert career, it would all have ended many years ago. It would be over now, done with, finished. So why live with regrets? What would you have now?" Without a moment's hesitation Dad replied, "Memories. I'd have memories." Well, he had me there. Instead of that gnawing feeling of an empty life he would have had fond recollections, poor soul.

In this regard, however, the mind often seems to be on automatic. I would rather think about my successes and happiness than brood about failures and regrets. Yet, the mind often turns to the latter. I think I know why. Its role is to guide us toward fulfillment. The successes are things already achieved, so no need to dwell on them, it says. It believes that the things that need attention are past failures and regrets. They must somehow be converted into something positive. So I reason. What do you think?

Of course I believe the only real and meaningful way to solve this problem is to have a nature imbued with bliss, bliss that will not be overshadowed by the dark moments and difficult days we all encounter. And we can gain this blissful state only when we are enlightened. And so we're back to basics. Go for it, I say, speaking of enlightenment. Plato did. And Socrates seems to have downed that ultimate cup of hemlock with a tranquil accepting, heart and mind, reflecting his high state of consciousness.

Why, I sometimes wonder, don't they give hemlock to those unfortunates who receive the death penalty in our criminal code? No one, I feel, has the right to take the life of another, but if the brutal sentence is to stand, at least let it be administered with a semblance of civility, rather than by savage hanging or crude electrocution. Why must society stoop to the same low level for which the accused is being punished?

"I think continually of those who were truly great," wrote poet Stephen Spender. As for me, I think often, if not continually, of those whose lives the society decided to end. Increasingly, modern scientific procedures show that individuals serve time for crimes they did not commit and sometimes give their lives for wrongs of which they were innocent.

Mary Suratt comes to mind, in whose house the Lincoln assassins hatched some of their plots and plans. The hysteria of the time led to her being hanged with other defendants on flimsy circumstantial evidence, a sad blot on the justice system of the time. Her poor 17-year-old daughter haunted the staircase that President Andrew

Johnson used to ascend to his White House bedroom. Ignoring her tearful pleas for the life of her mother, he resolutely passed her by.

My thoughts swiftly turn to the ill-fated Queen Marie Antoinette. I think she, too, got a bum rap. But, of course, in the overall cosmic scheme of things, maybe that was somehow in the cards for her. Just as it may be for the man who, while innocent, is convicted of a crime and serves, say 10 years. True, he did not commit that crime, but if nature made him serve 10 years there must have been a karmic reason, perhaps one dating back many years or even lifetimes. Absolute justice prevails in the world — at least according to numerous great sages of yesteryear and today.

It would perhaps be hard to explain that to, say, Herman Melville, author of *Moby Dick,* one of the acknowledged masterpieces of world literature. When it was published, the English critics, who then ruled the day, either trounced or dismissed it, while at home in America it sank almost without a trace. Melville's total earnings from his epic novel were a scant $556. In his later years he turned increasingly to poetry, writing some quite touching Civil War verse and, finally, a five-hundred-page epic poem called *Clarel,* about a student's pilgrimage to the Holy Land, a work that contains some of his deepest reflections. The long years he spent on it were rewarded with a reception even more chilling than that accorded *Moby Dick.* Ironically, in our time the respected critic Helen Vendler has expressed her admiration for this long-neglected work.

In the same vein, did I ever tell you the interesting question Deepak Chopra once asked of Maharishi Mahesh Yogi? "Maharishi," he began, "you are in a higher state of consciousness where you see the true reality of things. To many people the world today seems deeply troubled and even in misery. How does it look to you in your state?" Maharishi gave a swift simple answer — "Everything is as it should be." That puzzled Deepak, who at the time was helping Maharishi on numerous demanding projects. "But, Maharishi," he pursued, "if everything is as it should be, why are we working so hard to make things better?" "That," said Maharishi, "is also as it should be."

What do you think? I ask again. I value your opinion.

As for me, I do know this. When you learn Transcendental Meditation and start purifying your nervous system, your body rejoices and you see things differently. The mind clears up and turns ever more positive.

I'll give an example to which you can probably relate. Most everyone revolts against the older generation at a fairly early age. I did so to some degree but not until much later did I experience a major rebellion against my mother, so severe that one day I typed out a two-page, single-spaced blast which brought out all my negativity — how she had never given her children any expressed affection, how she charged the atmosphere of our house, how she had no sense of humor, and on and on.

Thank God I never mailed that poisonous missive — perhaps better spelled "missile." It would have destroyed a precious relationship, I feel sure. And happily, once I learned to meditate, my feelings toward my mother changed bit by bit until I found myself truly loving and appreciating her. Today my great regret is that I did not do more for her, did not tell her how much I cherished her, how I had come to revel in her sly sense of humor. She in turn delighted me one day when she was well over 90, saying, "You used to bring me wildflowers you picked along the railroad track, remember?" She certainly remembered that long ago gesture of my childhood. In her later years she always ended her letters to me by saying, "I love you very much." What a boon!

I'm reminded of a chat I once had with Barbara Walters. It came in the late 1960s when she was an anchor on NBC's *Today Show*, where she interviewed me for a book I had written called *Little Charley Ross: The story of America's first kidnapping for ransom.*

After the interview was over we had a pleasant talk about other books of mine, especially *The Child Stars*, where the longest chapter was on Judy Garland. Barbara's then husband, Lee Guber, had produced one of Judy's world tours. Barbara met her at this time and apparently Judy railed against her mom, who had indeed been a stereotypical stage mother, allowing MGM, her film studio, to put her on diet pills to slim down her chubby figure, sleeping pills so she could get to rest after arduous hours of filming, and amphetamines to revive her when she woke up drowsy.

Barbara agreed that Judy had legitimate complaints but she also felt strongly that one has to let go of childhood resentments at some point, certainly once one reaches adulthood. True, all too true, but without meditation, or some other profound stress-release modality, how can it be done?

17. Fun with Barbara Walters

By the way, I came to Transcendental Meditation by chance, pure luck, in 1972, at the ripe middle age of 45. At that stage of my life I did not consider myself a conscious spiritual seeker, my youthful aspirations in that direction at best on hold. I had just spent four or five years in Los Angeles working on my Hollywood books. Every day was enjoyable, I must say, especially conducting interviews with film people. Hold on! I forgot that I was telling you how I came to TM. Oh, well, we'll return to that subject in a bit and now I'll continue with more people I went to see for my film bios.

As a preface I want to point out that I was privileged to arrive in Hollywood in the 1960s when that legendary film capitol was in transition but still recognizable as a unique creative community, one big family. While several of the great studio heads had made their exit, some remained, and I went to see them. I talked to numerous gifted directors and studio craftsmen. "Pickfair," the fabled home of Mary Pickford, "America's Sweetheart," and her husband, Douglas Fairbanks, was still standing and on view to tourist buses, as was "Falcon Lair," the exotic den of Rudolph Valentino. I often walked by "Colonial House," where Bette Davis resided. I saw Cary Grant post a letter in a Beverly Hills mailbox, and glanced through a window of the Dome restaurant where Barbara Stanwyck was dining with a friend. "Sic transit Gloria Swanson," as someone has quipped. This sunset of the Hollywood of old was for me a striking adventure, another sweet taste of temporal Utopia.

I've already spoken of film figures I interviewed for my books, but here I'll cite Joseph Pasternak, who directed the popular Deanna Durbin pictures and also those of swimming champion turned film star Esther Williams. Not the greatest actress, Pasternak conceded, but added slyly, "Wet, she was a star." Certainly a good line, but I suspect he made liberal use of it over the years.

Mervyn LeRoy, who directed a long string of hits in addition to producing *The Wizard of Oz,* told me stories about them and showed me his beautiful house, a museum of rare Chinese artifacts of very ancient vintage. Impressive in a different vein was an interview with the founder of Paramount Pictures, Adolph Zukor, who had recently turned one hundred and was still completely clear-headed and forthcoming.

For the Hollywood books my publishers sometimes hired a publicity wizard named Jay Allen to take me around to talk shows and other interview venues in his sleek black Cadillac. He himself was a tall, imposing figure, always welcome at the Hollywood Brown Derby with one or another of his clients in tow.

Jay had only one client in each genre of entertainment. His male comic was wonderful, wry Paul Lynde whom I met and enjoyed, though when he was in his cups late of an evening he could be difficult, making a scene about the service in a restaurant, for example. Jay's female comedienne was delicious Kaye Ballard. He took me to see her in Las Vegas, where she held my hand after her show and said purringly, "Fa-a-a-mous author." That was an exaggeration, but nice just the same.

But let's return to the popular Brown Derby eatery, to use a term then in vogue. Jay invited me there one day along with Helen Gurley Brown, the highly successful editor of *Cosmopolitan* and author of the bestselling book, *Sex and the Single Girl.* When I asked this amiable lady if she could give my then current offering, *Garbo,* a plug in her magazine, she said, "Of course, Norman, since our two books are in no way competitive." She was true to her word.

The media whirl was often rich in incidents. I told you what Barbara Walters said about Judy Garland the day she interviewed me for the *Today Show* but I should also include the amusing prelude to the interview.

It took place at the NBC studio in New York quite early in the morning, as I recall. The first thing Barbara did was to show me a page of questions her staff had prepared for her. "What do you think?" she asked briskly. I looked over the list and replied, "I'm afraid they're rather boring." "I thought so," she said, and tore the sheet to shreds. "I haven't had time to read your book," she went on, "We'll have to wing it. What do you want me to ask you?" I told her to start by asking how I had come to write the book. That worked very well.

Now here's the amusing moment. While we were chatting I had the feeling that Barbara's leg was pressing against mine. Was it possible, I asked myself? Would this great lady be making a pass at me — at this bleak hour of the day? If it was true, and I didn't respond, would she give me a bad interview? On the other hand, if I responded, and had made a mistake, would I get an even worse outing? What a quandary! Just then I felt, very distinctly, the Walters gam pressing against my own.

"Norman, did you feel that?" she asked.

"Why, yes," I said sheepishly.

"When I do that during the interview," she breezed on, "it means I want you to finish your sentence quickly so we can break for a commercial. Got it?"

"Okay," I sighed with relief.

Happily, the interview went very well and Barbara said afterwards she wished we had had time for another segment. Later I wrote up this episode and sent it to the *Reader's Digest*, which ran it in its "Personal Glimpses" feature. I'm aware that the Walters interview took place in New York rather than Hollywood, which we were talking about, but that's how things go in conversation, isn't it? One thing just leads to another. So let's now go to other points east! Just as I became bi-coastal, so will you.

With my very first book, *The Child Stars*, I recall visiting Philadelphia to do the Mike Douglas talk show, a popular institution of the day. When I entered the elevator going up to the studio I saw that Mike was already inside, along with Jackie Coogan, who was to be one of the guests. Neither as yet knew who I was, so they spoke freely. I of course recognized Coogan from his immensely popular television comedy, *The Munsters*. For my book I had researched his equally successful career as a child star, most notably his big success at the age of five in *The Kid*, with Charlie Chaplin.

"What's all this child star crap?" I now heard him say to Mike Douglas.

"What's the matter?" said Mike. "Don't you want to talk about being a child star? What do you want to do? Do you want to sing? Do you want to dance?"

"Yeah," said Jackie. "I wanna sing. I wanna dance."

He did a little dance right there in that tiny elevator. Once the show got going he was completely loose, genial overall, and talked easily about his long successful life in show business. Apparently he had reconciled with his parents, who had managed, not always successfully, his finances in early years.

There was, however, one heart-thumping moment for me during the hour-long show when Mike pulled out a stack of child star photos and asked me to identify and comment on each one. Some of them were really minor figures and I could easily have come up dry, but fortunately I had done my homework and passed the test, identifying each photo and supplying a commentary.

Do you remember Phyllis Kirk, who was one of the stars of *The Thin Man* series on television? Later on she hosted a talk show for ABC and built one day's outing around *The Child Stars* and me. Guests included that lovely young actress, Carol Lynley, an even younger Brandon de Wilde, and Dickie Moore, who gave Shirley Temple her first on-screen kiss. Some years later I encountered Dickie Moore again after he had married another former child star, Jane Powell.

My book got a good deal of attention. The Doubleday Book Club picked it up and *Good Housekeeping* did a nice story on it. One evening I was featured on the popular *Long John Nebel Show*, which started in the evening and continued through the night, entertaining New York insomniacs until morning. Things were going very well when an unannounced visitor showed up.

Roddy McDowall had been listening to us on the radio, he said, and wanted to meet the author of *The Child Stars* because he thought it was the best book he had ever read about Hollywood. That was a splendid beginning for this unscheduled guest, but, alas, everything that followed was downhill for me.

Why? Roddy had recently taken up photography and was apparently very good at it. Long John Nebel was also a photography addict. For the next few hours these two talked shop and I moved to the periphery. Indeed, a few months later, when I was booked on *The Merv Griffin Show,* with Roddy as my co-guest, he had to cancel because *Life* magazine commissioned him to take photos of England's Princess Margaret during her visit to the United States.

I spoke to Roddy several times in later years and found him unfailingly gracious and helpful. My New York and Hollywood interviews turned up scurrilous stories about various celebrities but I never heard anything but praise for Roddy. During his last illness the press reported that he was seeing many guests and that one day Sybil Burton held his hand while seated on one side of his bed while Elizabeth Taylor, who had taken Sybil's place as Richard Burton's wife, sat holding his hand on the other, a touching tribute to his benign character and a life rich in friendship.

18. Laguna Beach and TM

The word friendship calls to mind once again my good pal Edith Bel Geddes, and another vacation trip we took to Mexico, once again to the palatial hacienda I described earlier. I bring up this second excursion because of an incident that occurred there and changed my life. As usual, the weather was perfect, the assorted company enjoyable, and the routine by now predictable. Wonderful walks or drives to picturesque nearby hamlets, ample hours for reading and swimming in a lovely pool, choice cuisine several times a day. While wine flowed freely at lunch, heavier beverages dominated the evening meal.

The day in question was like many others. I had downed a couple of manhattans, my libation of choice, and like everyone else I found my tongue tripping along most pleasantly. Edith was telling a story I had already heard many times, so I decided to slip away from the group and use the bathroom. There I was cleaning up when I looked in the mirror and quite unaccountably felt confused. You don't look happy, I thought to myself. You're in an earthly paradise but something's gone amiss. What's wrong? And suddenly I started to cry, softly at first, but soon reaching an operatic crescendo.

By now I knew what was wrong. Why do I have to keep repeating this routine, I asked myself. Surely there must be more to life than getting high, uttering a lot of nonsense that only seems humorous at the time, and waiting for the next morning's hangover. Fortunately the bad spell gradually passed. I dried my face and returned to join the others — and had another good stiff drink!

However, it was clear to me that something would have to be done. It took many months but eventually I left high-voltage New York for somewhat calmer California. I didn't turn teetotaler but at least I switched to wine. Eventually I decided that Hollywood parties were not too different from such gatherings in New York; the overall ambiance and the level of excitation were very similar. I felt the need for still more serenity.

As a reward for my productive years of work in West Hollywood I moved to beautiful Laguna Beach, about an hour south of Los Angeles, There I found a perfect little cottage on Bluebird Canyon and started turning my interviews into books. With no obligations to fulfill, I had time on my hands. When I saw a poster on a telephone pole announcing a lecture by Maharishi Mahesh Yogi I thought I'd wander by to see what he was like. See, just as promised, here's how I came to learn about meditation!

The talk turned out to be at a private house not far from my own, but there was certainly no one present who looked like a Maharishi. Perhaps a dozen people had already assembled when I arrived and a young man of about 18 was speaking. The poster apparently had said meditation "as taught by Maharishi." Well, it had been taught by Maharishi to this young man, who seemed very bright and cheerful. If I could be as happy as he was, I decided, perhaps I should try whatever he was doing.

A few weeks later I learned Transcendental Meditation, one-on-one, from him. It was nice, I thought, but not remarkable. Still, I continued day after day, so something good must have been happening. After several months I went to a weekend retreat where I enjoyed a more extensive meditation routine for the first time. Shortly thereafter the heavens opened up for me. I awoke each day feeling simply terrific. Every hour that followed was on that same high level of happiness.

For an entire year this state of euphoria persisted. Of course being in one of the great beauty spots of the world was a contributing factor. Laguna Beach has a superb climate and the scenic charm of the little village, comprising sixteen thousand inhabitants at the time, was staggering. The romantic Pacific Ocean daily caressed the lovely public beach and a dozen splendid coves all within easy walking distance. More than once I asked myself what I had done to deserve such bounty, such empyreal profusion.

Today, I believe that omniscient Mother Nature remembered my youthful spiritual stirrings even when I did not, and also noted my disillusion with metropolitan high life and my attempts to find a better road to fulfillment. This fellow is serious, she may have thought, so let's help him along with a nice meditation mantra. What do you think of these musings, dear one? I often try to imagine what Mother Nature is thinking. I hope she doesn't mind.

It was truly a hallowed time in lustrous Laguna. Eventually, however, though I still felt great, the glow of the new wore off somewhat. I was certainly living on a higher, better plane, and that persisted for years, but since it was routine, hence without much contrast, it was no longer so striking. Then, after a year in Europe on an advanced meditation course, I had a briefer but even deeper experience that I'll get to later. While what I've just described involved the glory of the relative, the later experience was more the glory of the absolute.

What's that? Ah, yes, you wonder about the absolute, or transcendent, which we've discussed several times. My Dad and I used to do it, too. "If the absolute is not material," he would say, "what is it? It's got to be something!" In my understanding, the transcendent lies at the deepest level of our mind. It's there in every person in the world but most people need a technique to access and/or taste it. I was so lucky to find TM at just the right moment. There's that lovely passage in Ecclesiastes: "To everything there is a season, and a time to every purpose under heaven."

Before this long and, I hope, agreeable detour, I believe we were talking about Judy Garland and her mother, and that makes me think of the equally interesting Ernest Hemingway and his mother. I've just started a book called *The Hemingway Women,* by Bernice Kert. It offers fascinating reading about Ernest's four wives, but also, for the first time, it gives a balanced picture of Grace Hemingway, his admittedly redoubtable mother. Yes, she had her faults, her weaknesses, her healthy self-esteem and self-concern, but she also had a great many good qualities, which the book brings out.

Hemingway could see little to admire in her and only a great deal to disparage, often exaggerating minor matters and neglecting the brighter side. In his adult years, those he met were often treated to diatribes against poor Grace. He would not, could not, let go of this animosity, not even at her death, when he failed to attend her funeral. Just to be fair, let me add that he was good with her in financial matters, signing over to her, for example, the handsome royalties for *The Sun Also Rises.*

19. A Near Death Experience

So I've pulled all these thoughts out of the memory bank. To me, it's simply astonishing how much of life consists of remembering things. My mind seems to be on a thought marathon, especially as I grow older. This is logical to some degree, since each year new things enter one's life and swell the memory bank.

I've read that the average person has over sixty-five thousand thoughts a day, certainly a whale of a lot of thoughts. And furthermore, ninety percent of these repeat from day to day. For a retired or inactive person the percentage must be even higher since less new data is coming in. So best be up and about, exploring fresh tracks. Stasis might well bring about boredom and depression, illness and you know what!

An astrologer once told me I would be able to choose the time of my departure from this world. I've long thought this may be so. Many decades ago, while living in New York, I had a near brush with death that was revealing in this regard.

I had gone to popular Jones Beach with a friend. While he visited with colleagues from his office I ventured out for a dip in the ocean, not realizing the tide was picking up. Suddenly an undertow swept me far out to sea. Naturally I felt a surge of terror, but the physical demands on me were so great that the moment passed. Since everyone else had swum to shore, I was alone, my cries for help unheeded.

I was, moreover, a mediocre swimmer, easily exhausted after a lap or two in a pool. Now I faced the mighty Atlantic Ocean. My intuition told me struggling would be counter-productive and fatal. My only chance for survival was to lie on my back and paddle to keep afloat.

This seemed to work, but just barely. Each new wave spilled billows of water over me, much of which went down my throat. I recall looking out to shore and seeing the beach crowd standing to watch my battle for survival. I had heard that moments like this made one's whole life flash through the mind. This did not happen to me. I saw those people on shore and thought, well, they will soon be going home and having cocktails, while I will be having —whatever I'm having who knows where.

I was getting more and more fatigued. I realized that I could let go. I could sink deep into the tiredness and accept death. But I did not. I decided to battle for my life with whatever strength I could still command. In the back of my mind the approaching cocktail hour may have played a role! Time passed, though I could not estimate its duration. I only recall that a brave young swimmer suddenly appeared, risking his life to try and save mine.

"Listen to me," he said, not yet coming too close. "I can help you, but you will have to do what I say. Will you listen and do what I tell you?"

"Ye-e-e-s," I managed to gurgle in his direction.

"If you panic and grab me, I'll have to slug you," he said, circling me. "You will drown. Got it?"

Again I gurgled fervently to obey him. And I did. He grasped one of my arms and started swimming to shore. Ever more forcefully the huge waves billowed over me and now I could not move to avoid them. Never, however, did I grab the dark-haired athlete who was saving my life. After a time a second rescuer came to help him.

Eventually we reached shore. I toppled down on the sand completely exhausted. The friend I had come with reappeared. He had not swum out after me, he said, because he was not a capable swimmer. My rescuing heroes disappeared into the crowd on the sands. Since I was no longer the star of an exciting event, no one now paid the slightest attention to me. The show was over. Believe me, I slept well during the night that followed.

More recently a second happening told me that I had a choice to go on living or accept a virtual sentence of death. I had radically changed my lifestyle, leaving behind a special meditation group I had known for decades and also moving from one part of the country to another.

The beauty of my new surroundings in the Napa Valley of California kept me amused and alert for a few months. I had checked into a handsome Veterans Home whose grounds were filled with trees transplanted from sites around the world. The costs of my stay were moderate, the food nourishing, with a good library right on the grounds, as well as other amenities. But then, once the novelty wore off, with no strong personal or work attachment, I found myself adrift, at sea, as it were, with little to do and too much time to do it in.

I awoke each day with a feeling of nausea and hopelessness. The denizens of the home, all military veterans, were uniformly pleasant but I was used to the fellowship of seekers on the spiritual path and missed them keenly. I knew it was just a matter of time before I would experience what Henry James, as noted, called "the distinguished thing." I would croak, to use a less luminous expression.

Once again I had a choice, whether to stay or to go. You can guess which path I chose. I opted for life, or as Milton so beautifully put it, "Off to fresh woods and pastures new!" Actually, I returned to the world of transcendental meditators in Iowa at Maharishi University of Management, where I found work in the public relations sector and good luck at every turn. I was born in Iowa, of course, and have long heard that one garners maximum support near the place of one's birth, rather a poetic concept.

Have you written any poetry? Has the muse ever touched you with a magic wand? She grazed me once upon a time, but not strongly enough to greatly influence my life. At an early age I fell madly and mysteriously in love. This bout of insanity, while only temporary, resulted in hours of coffee drinking and listening to Mozart piano concertos, all the while thinking of the beloved — and writing a poem a day! I tremble to think of those effusions now. At one point I tied them in a ribbon and gave them to a bewildered recipient, who soon after rejoined her family in Canada, surely a coincidence! Thank heaven I had not made copies.

I love the names of the nine goddesses who preside over literature and the arts in Greek mythology—Calliope, the muse of epic poetry; Clio, the muse of history; Erato, as you might guess, holds sway over erotic lyric poetry; Euterpe is the muse of music; Melpomene the muse of tragedy; Polyhymnia has charge of sacred poetry; Terpsichore of dance; Thalia of comedy; and Urania lords it over astronomy.

Somehow, for me, it's more pleasing to think of being ruled or influenced by gods and goddesses with colorful names than by impersonal laws of nature. So let's just capitalize 'gravity' and enjoy the heroic and resplendent powers of newly christened Gravity.

Quantum physicists say our whole universe is constructed of sounds or vibrations, starting with the Big Bang. There's a romantic concept for you! Of course I missed that Big Bang by I don't know how many billion years — or maybe trillions?

20. Blissful Days, Painful Regrets

Fortunately I have had some experiences of the absolute level of life. In 1978, after a year of advanced Transcendental Meditation courses in Switzerland under Maharishi's direct guidance, I returned home to teach TM in Cedar Falls, Iowa. I must have brought back some of the deep silence, coherence, and harmony pervading those courses because everything went so smoothly, almost effortlessly.

After working in the local meditation center all by myself for some six months, teaching over a hundred people how to transcend, it happened. I fell into a state I can only describe as ecstasy. Every moment of every day was permeated with profound bliss and I was keenly aware of it. No doubts and no questions about the purpose of life, or anything else, troubled me. Everyone and everything seemed to be infused with the divine. Everything was as it should be.

I vividly recall going to the University of Northern Iowa's Student Center where a TV was tuned to a gala celebration of some country's anniversary. Stars of stage, screen, and opera performed to great applause but whenever there was praise for them or the theme of the evening I inwardly repeated, "No, no, no! Praise only the divine, the infinite, the eternal, blissful Creator! Praise only God!"

This glorious state lasted several weeks and then the cloth of life that had been dyed such a bright hue began to fade. The decline was so gradual that my physiology and consciousness were able to cope. My normal state was still a good place to be — and I now knew once and for all what it was like to live in the grace of God. That episode has sustained me through all the years that followed.

I've had other radiant experiences but that was the best. What was your peak experience in this lifetime? When you start thinking about it, you may be pleased at what you come up with. So-called peak experiences are not that unusual. At its best, what splendor this human physiology is capable of!

However comforting my life resume may be, my thoughts still sometimes wander in the direction of things I missed, passed on, or neglected. Perhaps I should give more concrete examples of this masochistic mania.

I'll begin with a luncheon in Paris in 1962 that was arranged for me to meet the celebrated French writer Jean Cocteau, whom I had long admired. Author of novels like *Les Enfants Terribles,* auteur of films still viewed as classics like *Beauty and the Beast,* Cocteau, while no longer in his prime, was still a prominent figure on the French cultural scene. My friend Herve Mille, editor of *Paris Match,* thought that I might want to commission an article from him for *Theatre Arts,* with which I was then affiliated.

Why did I skip a gourmet meal at a four-star French restaurant with this man I greatly admired? Ah, here comes the embarrassing part, which I only reluctantly relate. I had just finished a vacation trip to Turkey and Greece, catching cold in the process. To get over it, I downed some drinks the night before the meeting, followed by more than a swig of savory sauterne. In the morning I felt wiped out and still in the grip of a cold. And while it was April in Paris, it was also cold in Paris, and damp in Paris. And, more than anything, I wanted to be back in New York in my own warm flat.

So, on a flimsy pretext, I canceled lunch with Cocteau and flew home. I was thoroughly selfish and one big fool. And here I am living with this nagging regret. Alas, I could recount other such dilemmas.

I once turned down a trip along the historic Hudson River because I was on a special meditation course and enjoying it. I feared that leaving for a week might wipe out the benefits I had just gained. Similarly, I canceled a week with friends from Cornell College, thus missing a stay on lovely Lake Cayuga. High on my list of regrets is an all-expense-paid trip to the chateau country of France, which I turned down because I was undergoing a purification process for my addled physiology and feared the rich French cuisine would stunt my progress.

There have been many other occasions in my life that I botched. Always there were good rationales for doing so at the time, but oh how I now wish I had lived it up. Carpe diem!

In the emotional realm, which I have touched on, I passed over many promising relationships, viewing as a goose anyone who seemed to like me. At some level, I suspect, my self-esteem was low, and nipped these encounters in the bud, while a fear of committing myself jinxed others. Only years later did I fully realize how nutty I had been. When I described the dilemma to a friend and asked why I did these things, he said just one word, "Perverse." Fortunately, I did also have periods of sanity.

Now let's move on to the encounters where I actually hurt people, by sins either of commission or omission. I'll only mention two or three, because it's just too painful for me to recall these failings in myself.

While living in New York in the 1960s I was invited for the weekend to Fire Island Pines by a nice lady friend. I was planning to stay through Sunday and return Monday morning but one of the other guests asked if I'd like to join him for dinner on Long Island at the estate of a wealthy friend, who, in turn, was a friend of the Duke and Duchess of Windsor. The Duchess was a contemporary heroine to me, the woman for whom a king of England, no less, had given up his throne. I jumped at the chance to hear stories about her.

Rather casually I told my hostess I would be leaving Sunday afternoon to go back to the city, which disappointed her since she expected guests to stay one more night and it now turned out everyone was going back, leaving her alone in the house. I could have passed on this tempting dinner invitation. Did I? No, I did not. It was graceless on my part, since I owed allegiance for the weekend to her, but the deed was done. I went to the dinner on Long Island to hear tales about the Duchess. How were they? There were none. Her name never came up.

Here's another thing I did that was far worse. While at the University of Iowa in 1953, getting my Master's Degree in English Literature, I met a young girl from the Deep South and started dating her. We were usually laughing because she had a fine sense of humor, but we were also participating in the dating ritual and pecking each other on the cheek to end our meetings.

Then one evening there was an abrupt change. We were sitting and laughing, but less than usual. Tenderly, wistfully, she took my hand. She apologized for being so serious, she said, but she had just heard that day that her brother, who was in the army, had been killed in a training accident. When I put my arm around her to console her she responded with what I can only describe as abandon. It became obvious that she wanted to make love.

In retrospect, I can understand. The confrontation with death can easily lead to a desire, probably quite unconscious, to engage in the sexual act, to go through the ritual of mating which results in giving birth, thus triumphing over death. In a novel by Emile Zola, a man and woman working in a grain elevator suddenly realize that something has gone wrong with the machinery and they are about to be buried by the pouring grain. Primitive emotions overtake them both as they desperately copulate — and die.

Well, I wasn't up to the needs this sorrowing girl had. I was frightened. I withdrew from the closeness of the moment and let the evening come to an end. I allowed the relationship, too, to wither because I was out of my depth at the time. And so I must have left a bruise, one of which I am deeply ashamed.

What do you think of these revelations? Do they resonate or are they way off base to you? I certainly don't want to give the impression that I've only done foolish or selfish things. From a very early age I had the desire to make things better in the world. Here's a rather amusing illustration. I was no more than six or seven when a distant relative came to visit. He arrived, moreover, in a wheelchair, having suffered some accident that made it a necessity. This touched me. I felt the need to act and began to correspond with him. The poor man may well have quaked when he saw my childish scrawls in the mailbox, but he dutifully answered over quite a period of time.

Overall, I'm quite even tempered and often think of others. I'm happy to help friends when they go through emotional turmoil. I will make a concerted effort to guide unemployed friends toward a better job. I choose gifts with care. I won't offer examples because I don't think routine good deeds are particularly interesting. As Tolstoy said in this vein, happy families have no history, meaning they're all alike.

21. Jokes and Quotations

As I go on with this narrative of memories and reflections, I think more and more of you out there taking it all in. I see you as bright, discriminating, and well disposed toward others and indeed all mankind. Naturally, I would like to please you. And here I have to make decisions. Just how far should I go when it comes to the warts in my nature? You may recall that Henry Fonda — along with many others — once said he wanted his life story to be told "warts and all." It's easy to say that when someone else is doing the telling for you, but when you yourself are at the keyboard, singing the song of your life, it becomes a challenge. Too many warts and you could go off-key.

Have you noticed in your own life how treacherous praise and blame can be? Just yesterday someone left a copy of *Vanity Fair* at my door. It was not in the usual wrapper but in a plain envelope with my name on it. So how did my subscription copy get from my open mail slot to my residence door? Obviously, thought I, some eager beaver could not resist reading my copy before I got to it. I was quite annoyed with this person, probably someone living in the same building with me, hence the hand delivery.

My feelings of annoyance were growing when a friend asked if I had found the copy he had left for me, his own subscription copy. It was someone I knew only casually who did me this kindness, un-aware that I already subscribed. My nasty thoughts about some villain lifting — nay, stealing — my subscription copy were way off base. It arrived the following day.

Shame for my unjustified negativity came over me, of course. Many years ago I counseled myself to think of the x-factor in these situations, to make allowance for the unknown. I should have listened to myself!

On a more cheerful note, I love this jolly story that someone just sent me. The Mother Superior says to her flock, "It is my task to tell you there is a case of gonorrhea in the house." "Wonderful," exclaims an elderly sister in the back of the hall, "I was getting awfully tired of the Chardonnay."

Have I told you that I think Beatrice Lillie was one of the funniest ladies of all time? Never heard of her, eh? Before your time, eh? Well, so was Abraham Lincoln but surely you've heard of him! Anyhow, the favorite story of the great English comedienne goes this way. A young man knocks at the porch door of a little old lady who answers, saying "Yes?" "I'm from the West Staffordshire high school band," he chirps. "We're raising money for new uniforms. Can you help?" "What's that?" she replies, cupping one ear with her hand. He repeats. And she repeats. He asks a third time, and she replies a third time. "I'm afraid my hearing is off today," she says. "We'll have to give it up." He reluctantly bows, climbs down the steps, walks along the sidewalk to the property gate, which he neglects to close behind him. "Mind the gate," comes her voice from on high. "F— the gate," he mutters, remembering her deafness, and marches on, only to hear her shrill rejoinder swirling down from the porch — "And f— the West Staffordshire high school band!" Mind you, I'm paraphrasing from memory but that is the gist of the joke.

This might be a good time to pause for a reflection on citations like the one I just attributed to Beatrice Lillie, that magician of laughter I was fortunate enough to see on Broadway in the 1950s. I quote a fair number of other people during the course of this memoir. Some readers may quibble about the exact wording in some instances and also about the attribution of quotes.

I will refer them to a fine reference work called *Mark My Words,* a six-hundred page compendium of quotes and attributions compiled by Nigel Rees, who devised and for decades presided over a BBC radio program called *Quote…Unquote.* What emerges from those pages is the tricky and elusive nature of quotes, including very familiar ones. The exact words of many quotes are hard to pin down, and often there is no reliable source for the attribution.

Familiar quotes tend to cling, barnacle like, to certain personalities. In his day, Samuel Goldwyn was often credited with malapropisms that he had not coined. Since he reveled in publicity, he did not correct these misattributions. Oscar Wilde and George Bernard Shaw did indeed originate many wonderful quotes and as a consequence a second wave, not their own, gravitated to their names.

Mae West, W.C. Fields, and Groucho Marx probably harvested such additions, along with humorists Robert Benchley, George S. Kaufman, and Dorothy Parker. Today, Woody Allen has certainly spawned some good quotes and as a result will surely inherit a few more. The witty and wise Kaufman once commented, "Everything I've ever said will be credited to Dorothy Parker." Somehow my mind goes to Claude Rains, playing a military official in *Casablanca,* and telling his subordinates, "Round up the usual suspects."

I'm pleased to report that I'm quoted twice in *Mark My Words,* once under the Greta Garbo entry for confirming that during a salary argument with her MGM boss, Louis B. Mayer, she uttered the classic sentence, "I tank I go home," and again under the Sam Goldwyn entry, confirming that he said, "Anyone who goes to a psychiatrist needs to have his head examined."

While writing my own books I sometimes interviewed several people who were present at some incident in the making of a movie. In consequence I had three or four versions of what happened. Depending upon the context, I sometimes used all four, but then again I might use only the one I thought best. History can be elusive, don't you think? The victor tells his tale, while the vanquished tells quite another.

22. The French and Joie de Vivre

Before I return, very briefly, compulsively, to regrets in my life, I'll counter with some of my happy days in France, from 1951 to 1953. In Paris I made friends early on with a genteel young lady at the Alliance Française who called me one day to see if I'd like to tutor someone in English, a French personage of quite a high station in life. I'd be well paid.

Of course I was eager to hear what she was offering me. Anne Marie, my friend, said I was to have breakfast three days a week at the Élysée Palace, residence of the President of France! My repast would be with his son, Paul, who was in his forties, already spoke English, but wished to become more fluent in his role as secretary to his father.

I should indicate that the President at the time was Vincent Auriol, then in his 70s and often called "Papa Auriol" by his compatriots. Mind you, General Charles de Gaulle was waiting in the wings but not quite ready to move center stage.

I was living in a nice little hotel near the Luxembourg Gardens and soon, three mornings a week, an official limousine from the Élysée would come to pick me up. It made quite an impression on the proprietor of the Hotel Racine, who watched as we sped off, the French tricolor showing the way.

Paul Auriol was a gracious host, receiving me in the lobby of the historic and ornate royal residence, guiding me to the family apartment, where he lived with his father, his wife Jacqueline, a famed French aviatrix, and their children. At first Paul would ask what I wanted for breakfast in French but soon we were debating the merits of toast versus croissants in English. He already knew the language quite well, so it was simply a matter of making his speech more relaxed, and that came naturally. From time to time I would receive a sealed envelope with my remittance.

The highlight of the year came one day when Paul pointed at a television set in our breakfast area. "Do you have one in your hotel?" he queried. When I said no, he asked if I would like to join him and view the coronation, to take place the following day, of England's Queen Elizabeth II. No, I said, I was busy with a tennis engagement. Just joking.

I was elated, of course. The very next day I was invited to the family's inner sanctum. I was introduced to Papa Auriol, who greeted me warmly, then popped in and out of the room during the colorful ceremony while also tending to state business. Later, when I finished my teaching assignment in France, I wrote up this adventure, calling it "Breakfast at the Élysée," and sold it to the *American Mercury*, which was then edited by the great H. L. Mencken near the end of his rich and fruitful life.

Since I spoke in passing of General de Gaulle, I'd like to express here my great admiration for that noble statesman, who rescued France from a second-tier status and restored her grandeur. Of course Churchill said that of all the crosses he had to bear, the cross of Lorraine, meaning General de Gaulle, was the heaviest. Churchill could be very incisive, but Charles de Gaulle was no slouch in this department either, as witness his oft quoted remark about his native land: "How can you govern a country that produces 246 different kinds of cheese?"

This brings to mind the objective correlative, that one act or gesture that completely expresses the essence of an individual. The example often given is that of Flaubert's Madame Bovary using her delicate tongue to reach the bottom of her sherry glass and capture the last drop.

Here's a moment that encapsulates a facet of General de Gaulle's character that is not generally known. He and his wife Yvonne had a son and two daughters, one of whom was mentally impaired and died at the end of her teens. At the ceremony that marked her passing the General gently put his arm around his wife and was heard to say, "Now she is like the others." Was this not the most thoughtful reflection possible?

For Madame de Gaulle I would cite the time she and the General were out driving when an assassin fired bullets at their limousine and the occupants only escaped death because the windshield, though scarred, was bulletproof. After the chauffeur deposited the couple at the Élysée, the General offered his arm to his wife. She took it and together they calmly made their way inside, where a reporter said, "Madame, it was such a dangerous moment and yet you seem so calm." "Yes," she replied with great simplicity, "but remember, we are old, so it is not so serious, and we were together." Again, it seems to me this was the perfect expression for a major moment in a life. Vive la France!

My days in France, now 50 years distant, have never left me. Click goes a part of my brain and I'm carting home a baguette of fresh French bread and a bottle of Beaujolais. Click and I'm in the chateau country, visiting Chambord and Chenonceaux with a lovely French family that all but adopted me. Click and I'm in Paris at the Comedie Francaise, listening to the magical language of the great French dramatist Racine. I can still smell the bread, see the noted double staircase at Chambord, and hear again the glorious verse of Racine declaimed by celebrated actress Marie Bell. The visionary Utopia comes in many forms, spiritual and earthly. For me, my sojourn in France was one of the best of the latter.

While we're dwelling on the virtues of French culture, I submit that a fine antidote to regrets and depression may be hearing Edith Piaf sing *Je ne regrette rien*. Recordings are easily available, but this is a good time to recall the night that I heard the little sparrow, "le petit moineau," as she was called, in person.

I've already told you that on one of my first navy leaves, or liberties, I flew from my post at the Great Lakes Naval Training Center to

New York, hoping to hear Ethel Merman blast out the great Irving Berlin songs in *Annie Get Your Gun*.

After this terrific theatre experience I was wandering the streets of New York's fashionable East Side when I came across the Club Versailles, where a discreet marquee said that Edith Piaf was appearing, supported by a male group called "Les Compagnons de la Chanson."

The *maître d'* informed me, however, that all the tables were taken, as well as the seats at the bar. What to do? "Un moment," he said, and spoke to a managerial looking type, who cast a glance my way, noted my uniform, and smiled. The *maître d'* returned and told me he would seat me on stage just out of sight but well within hearing.

The entire show was magical. Piaf, petite, well under five feet short, was dressed in a plain black dress. Her voice made up for the diminutive stature as it soared with each emotional lyric. She sang plaintively of love lost, but also poignantly of love restored. *Je ne regrette rien* and *La vie en rose* lingered in one's memory. My offer to pay for the privilege accorded me that notable night was brushed aside.

Happily, this was no isolated experience. When I first went to France in 1951 on my French Government Teaching Assistantship, I was instantly treated with that same unfailing courtesy. I've already talked about Paris adventures, but my first year in France was actually spent in the south, in the handsome city of Bordeaux, where not many people spoke English, so it was sink or swim. I swam and was often thought to be French, or perhaps Belgian-French, so rapidly did I progress. Since the English classes I taught were voluntary, students came the first week to check out the new American instructor and never showed up again. As a result I had plenty of time to explore the surrounding countryside and the excellent local wines.

When I requested a transfer to Paris for my second year, the official in charge said he would do what he could, and then added, "Mais une belle fille ne peut donner que ce qu'elle a." — "But a beautiful girl can only give what she's got." Don't you love that piquant expression? In Paris, by contrast with Bordeaux, one heard English at every turn.

There it would have been far more difficult for a foreigner to become fluent in French. Here's a closing tip. If you want to learn a new language, memorize the nation's popular songs. It's a pleasant shortcut to fluency. I used Edith Piaf songs in this way, improving my French while ingesting her ardent philosophy of life.

23. What to Do with a Leftover Life

In this regard, my friend Charley Lutes used to say, "When you're unhappy, think happiness. It won't make you happy but it will derail the negative thoughts. When they come back you'll have to do it once more, and when they come back again, ditto." Well, you can say that again!

Charley Lutes is not a name that will be familiar to you. I feel I was lucky to know him. When we first met he was in thriving middle age, a handsome, tall man with a matinee-idol profile. At one point in his life he tried to get into motion pictures but missed a chance for stardom when a young William Holden grabbed a much-coveted role.

Charley became a successful business executive and helped found the TM offspring Spiritual Regeneration Movement, guiding its destinies from a hall in West Los Angeles where he held regular Sunday afternoon meditation sessions attended by numerous Hollywood celebrities, including the then upcoming film director David Lynch, whose stature grew rapidly with *Eraserhead, Blue Velvet, Elephant Man,* and later, *The Straight Story* and *Mulholland Drive. Twin Peaks,* his foray into television, was an immediate success.

He recently became very public about his zeal for TM and launched a non-profit foundation to bring it to at-risk school children around the world. When he and his friend, legendary singer/songwriter Donovan, made a tour of US cities for the foundation, their reception at each venue was phenomenal. David is clearly a cultural icon, revered for his stunning originality. His recent book, *Catching the Big Fish* — the fish a symbol for creativity — reached bestseller lists in numerous cities.

Not long ago he visited Maharishi University, where I presently work in the media office, and one day, leaving a school building, I saw him standing alone in a quiet recess, looking out at the grounds. I thought of speaking to him, telling him that I was helping to get articles into the press about his foundation, but I decided not to interrupt his musings, his privacy.

I think celebrities are often conflicted about this aspect of their lives. They want the public recognition their work has brought them but sometimes they fight off their fans. I recall years ago an afternoon at Sardi's in New York. A business lunch had taken me there and almost everyone had left when suddenly there was a commotion near the entrance. All remaining eyes turned in that direction and I recognized Basil Rathbone, best known for his screen portrayal of Sherlock Holmes. He was with a party of friends and loudly proclaiming, "Find a corner for us, won't you. We want quiet, quiet, quiet!" Each "quiet" was louder than the last. "We need privacy!" he added in stentorian tones. Ironically, of course, had he been more subdued he would have had his wish. Or would he?

Was he completely aware of what he was doing, do you think? Was it a performance? Or was his surface level of behavior at odds with his true desires? I know that I have often behaved in a manner that was quite out of tune with my deepest desires. I would say things that seemed okay at the moment, only to realize later that I had acted against my own interest.

As I think about these matters I am constantly forced to revert to the past. Thinking about bygone days takes up a good proportion of my time. Does it do so for yours? I'm not keen on this. While I'm reliving the past, trying to figure it out, the present is slipping away. The fact that I close my eyes twice a day to meditate probably accentuates this tendency. Of course I don't want to abandon meditation and throw out the baby with the bath water, but I am faced with a dilemma.

I also assume that writing down these reminiscences is acting as a further stimulus to the memory bank. What I should probably do to get away from this trap is to engage in some completely new activity. Something really refreshing would probably add years to my life, and I'd like another decade to add to my 80-plus years. Why don't I just pack up and head for Milton's fresh woods and pastures new? I've already told you about the experiment that took me to California's Napa Valley but failed despite the beauty that surrounded me.

Where would I go this time and why don't I just start something new here in tiny but resourceful little Fairfield, Iowa, home of Maharishi University of Management and therefore awash in young students with innovative thoughts and peppy plans for each day?

Well, there are two compelling reasons to contemplate leaving this admitted haven. With all its undeniable assets, Fairfield is not a scenic wonderland, though quite okay, and the climate can be severe, not excessively so but enough to make one think at times of going elsewhere.

The first alternative is the lure of foreign locales, maybe France where I lived so happily for two years half a century ago, or exotic Venice, or the Italian Riviera, or…. No, stop. I want to make a new start, but going abroad in one's 80s, and during these stormy modern times, would really be too much of a challenge.

In the USA, the first choice for another experiment would again be California, maybe beautiful Laguna Beach, where I spent such a happy decade in the 1970s. The trouble is — and there are question marks everywhere, it seems, as I muse about this predicament — the trouble with Laguna Beach is that while I was happy there long ago, I left because things were changing. All my friends were moving to Iowa to be near the heart of the TM Movement and I felt so lonely without them that I left to join them.

If I went back now I would feel isolated and lonely again, only more so. As Thomas Wolfe said, "You can't go home again." You can go, but you probably won't like it. It will have changed, and in most cases not for the better.

I could go to some entirely new place. Since I've always liked university towns because they have bright young people with a forward impetus, maybe I could make a go of it in Eugene, Oregon; or in Sacramento, California, near Mount Shasta, said to be a spiritually awake area; or perhaps Boulder, Colorado, would be a happy haven. On the other hand — I seem to have lots of these hands — I don't know anyone in any of the three and starting over on my own might be rough.

In younger years I would have taken up the challenge without much urging. I remember when living at home again in Iowa after getting a B.A. from Harvard College, I packed a bag and went to California as easily as one goes to the market. I hadn't decided what to do with myself so I found a room in Berkeley, checked in at the local Harvard Club, since I was now a graduate, and was told by a job counselor that I could go to an insurance company as a trainee or do social work for a government agency. I decided my future was not in insurance, tried the social work and realized that it was not to be my life either, and wondered if Europe held the answer I sought. Again I packed my bag and blithely took the Queen Mary to England. It was all so easy to move around in those days.

Since I now cling rather tenaciously to my modest haven in Iowa, why not make the best of it and stay, accepting the rather tough climate and the lack of anything approaching the beauty of Lake Titicaca or Mount Everest — or even Grant's Tomb! Just kidding there. What do you think, bright one? You're a veteran of your own circuitous and sometimes snarled saga of life. Where should I ask the shifting sands of time to plunk me down? Mull it over, dear, and let me know what you recommend.

While you're mulling though, let me add that there are additional challenges for me here in Fairfield that you might consider. While I would have spasms of loneliness in a new and distant domicile, I have them here, too. I seem to veer between spells of agreeable seclusion and bouts of conviviality. I'm a gregarious hermit. The problem arises because when I'm feeling reclusive I put off my friends and find excuses for passing on their invitations. Then, when I'm feeling forlorn and seek them out, they are sometimes less than enthusiastic.

I'm reminded of playwright George S. Kaufman, who liked to dine very early. One evening a friend called him around 8 o'clock and asked what he was doing about dinner. "Digesting it," replied gallant George.

Oh, what's the use! Although the matter is far from settled, I'll probably stay in this little cocoon until I'm booted out. I've heard that Mother Nature does that when you've accomplished whatever you were supposed to do in any given place. When you've learned your lesson, you move on, or else! What about you? Do you believe that life is a school and that we're here to learn lessons through one little, or one big, test after another? It kind of makes sense to me.

24. Favorite Poems and Prose

I have a confession to make. Throughout this kaleidoscopic conversation with you I've gone easily from subject to subject, never at a loss for what comes next. Right now, however, my mind is pleasantly vacant. Oops, here comes a thought, and I think a good one. I feel the need for something wholesome, and sweet, and uncomplicated.

I therefore offer a poem by Leigh Hunt entitled *Jenny Kissed Me*. Do you know it? I like it partly because it's about something that really happened. Leigh Hunt knew many of the great poets of the Romantic era, the likes of Keats and Shelley, and also Thomas Carlyle and his appealing wife Jane — Jenny to intimates — who were his neighbors in London's Chelsea district. After a bout of illness, Hunt felt strong enough to go next door to renew his friendship with them. The celebrated poem was the result of that visit. Here it is:

> Jenny kissed me when we met,
> Jumping from the chair she sat in.
> Time, you thief, who love to get
> Sweets into your list, put that in:
> Say I'm weary, say I'm sad,
> Say that health and wealth have missed me,
> Say I'm growing old, but add
> Jenny kissed me.

To be sure, there's an engaging postscript as well. While Thomas and Jane were both superior beings, they could be as difficult as they were gifted. This prompted a wag to say the heavens were kind when they had these two marry, since it made only two people miserable out of a possible four!

So, refreshed, we return to what I should do with my leftover life. It's not an easy thing to answer. I have certain limitations, wherever I land. Many people find the days too short. I sometimes do, too, but at other times I find them rather long. You see I don't play bridge or any other games. I don't play tennis or any other sports, though I do follow the Chicago Cubs in baseball, a daunting challenge since anyone who nibbles at that franchise turns into a lifer. Enough of what I don't do.

I do enjoy reading, especially biographies. Somerset Maugham said that for some people reading was a pleasant occasional diversion. For him, he added, it was a necessity, like bread and butter. It's like that for me. I read at least an hour each day, sometimes two. I like to escape from my own life for a while and enter someone else's. Ah, yes, you probably wonder what biographies I would recommend.

I'll start with Henri Troyat's *Tolstoy,* a behemoth of a book about an inspiring epic figure. We all know about his magnificent literary output and his powerful social and political activism, which made him a hero to many, but all his days he felt guilty about his privileged status and finally, in his 80s, this grand old man supplied a perfect coda for his life. He packed a bag, leaving everything behind, and set out to follow the path of a mendicant. What incredible courage. Well, maybe he had his manservant pack the bag, and maybe the manservant accompanied him, but never mind, he was great in every sense of the word.

Here's a curious coincidence. Listening to the radio last night I learned that at a performance of Tchaikovsky's *D Major String Quartet* — the one containing the grand "Andante Cantabile" which inspired the song *June on the Isle of May* — Tolstoy was seated next to the composer, who was treated to the sight of the great man moved to tears by his music.

Since writers themselves often put Henry James atop their list of best loved authors, lives of this singular figure are numerous. I tip my hat to a four-volume biography by Leon Edel but I prefer the much shorter work of H. Montgomery Hyde, who captures James's lovable personality in a most engaging manner.

A major work about a celebrity, a screen star no less? Yes, why not? I recommend *Marlene Dietrich,* by her daughter, actress Maria Riva. Her closeness to her subject makes the anecdotes intimate, embarrassingly so at times, but with an overriding respect and admiration. Dietrich comes across as fascinating, outrageous, generous and brave, a marvelous self-creation. Her daughter captures it all.

My last choice, for now, is a sleeper that wins you over by taking a virtually unknown figure and making you wonder why no one discovered her long ago. In *Misia: The Life of Misia Sert,* the gifted classical piano duo Arthur Gold and Robert Fizdale took on their task with knowing research and hearty gusto. Of Polish-Russian-French ancestry, Misia Godebska was a gifted pianist and also comely, vivacious, and quite droll. She was married several times, most notably to the Spanish painter Jose Maria Sert, who did designs for Diaghilev's Ballet Russes. Most of her life was spent in Europe, where she knew and charmed a stellar avant-garde set that included Claude Debussy and Maurice Ravel, who dedicated "La Valse" to her; Renoir and Toulouse Lautrec, who painted her portrait; and Stephane Mallarme and Jean Cocteau of the literary world. *Misia,* in turn, charmed me and will probably do the same for you.

Speaking of Cocteau reminds me once more of that engagement to meet him for lunch, foolishly canceled by me. I could slap myself for having done so. There, I just did! I seem to have quite a list-making tendency in my life — the people I've loved best, the regrets I have, and here comes another one. I've made a little list of odd fragments of my life that keep recurring in my thoughts for no good reason that I can determine.

As an example, there's the name Betty Selden. Years ago I found it in an old address book and tried to recall why it was there. I vaguely remember meeting a young woman by that name and obviously knew her well enough to put it in my address book. Since I never called her over many decades, why call her now? The question is mute. Her name has disappeared from my more recent phone and address books.

It obviously remains in my memory bank, however, because every now and then it flits through my mind. Each time this happens I ask a blessing for her. By now quite a shower must have rained down on her, wherever she may be. Betty, are you still there?

25. Dylan Thomas, Eliot, Cummings

A nd you, my dear reading aficionado, are you still there? We've known each other for a good while now, maybe three or four months. You've heard a bunch of my stories and there are more, I assure you, new ones you might like. To use my old metaphor, many petals of the rose have unfolded, throwing light on my life, and more await you to complete the process. But remember this is just a book. You can put it down now for good — or you can pick it up again a little later. It's for you to decide!

What? Oh, I'm so glad you're planning to stay around. You seem to be hiding some quite fascinating things about yourself but you have a nice accepting nature that I've gotten used to. If you'd gone away I would have missed you!

And right off I want to report something Maharishi said on a video I saw recently. It was late in the evening and I was starting to doze off when my ear caught the phrase "two-hundred percent of life." Use TM to infuse the transcendent into your nervous system, he advised, and continue until it's present one hundred percent of the time. The refined state of consciousness that ensues, he said, will enable you to experience the material realm in all its glory, giving you a second hundred percent of life. What a joyous prospect! And who ever said you can't have your cake and eat it, too!

Now, is it okay if I drop another name, or two, or three? How about leading off with Dylan Thomas? It's the early 1950s and I'm living in Iowa City, getting a Master's Degree in English Literature at the University of Iowa.

Between classes I stop in at the student-faculty lounge for coffee when in walks Dylan Thomas, short and cherubic but looking a bit bedraggled. He's in town for a reading and is known to keep late hours at the parties given for him. At these he is not always on his best behavior, drinking at a fast clip and making rash proposals to cute faculty wives. With no one else in the lounge, we start talking about Laurence Olivier's new film and other topics in the cultural news. He seems content with easy chitchat and says he misses his children, telling me their lovely Welsh names, which I cannot recall, but will look up this very minute. Ah, yes, Llewelyn, Aeronwy, and Colm. I remember that he said with some emotion, "They're what make it all worthwhile."

The next day I went to hear him read, mostly his own works, but also some by fellow bards. At one point he said, "I am now going to recite a poem by Robert Browning." Pause. "There's one good line in it." Pause. "It's by Christopher Marlowe." Laughter. Twice during the session he left the podium and sauntered over to a drinking fountain. After several good gulps he rewarded himself with a hearty burp.

Staying with the bards, I go back to my Harvard College years where I recall most pleasantly Marianne Moore and T.S. Eliot. Wearing her signature tri-cornered hat, Marianne read several short poems and seemed to be just hitting her stride when, to my surprise, she grabbed her papers and marched down the aisle and out. T. S. Eliot was very suave indeed, rather tall and wearing a well-cut suit with a handkerchief tucked into his left shirtsleeve. It was used to dab his brow during the very clipped English-accented version of *The Hollow Men,* ending so soulfully, "This is the way the world ends, this is the way the world ends, not with a bang but a whimpuh!"

Before I go on about other poets, I want to tell a story on myself. When I drop names of prominent figures I've known, most people are interested and accepting but occasionally a friend feels I've gone too far, though I'm only talking about what happened in my life, something I really can't change. Anyhow, one fellow, still a good friend today, did tire for a while of hearing about my celebrity encounters. During this particular week our discussion turned to religion and spirituality. I recall that at one point I said, "But God is omnipotent."

"Well, you would know, wouldn't you?" he snapped. "You met him, of course, didn't you? You two hit it off, right?" Curiously, on one level that was true, though it was not a street encounter but something on a deeper level, as I've indicated.

Returning to the beguiling subject of poets, when I went to New York in 1956 to start my magazine and writing career, I got a call from my friend, poet Paul Engle, director of the University of Iowa's fabled literary workshops. He was a regular visitor to New York and on this occasion he was going to stop by to see his colleague, E. E. Cummings, and would I like to come along?

Yes, said I, and off we went to Patchin Place, in Greenwich Village, where cummings — who, as you know, did not like caps — lived. I was introduced and acknowledged in a congenial manner. The greeting I returned was the only participation required of me during this half-hour visit. Paul and his chum did the talking, almost entirely a catch-up conversation. Then Cummings led Paul and me out to the street, stopping at one point to shout at the window of another of the flats, "Are you still alive, Djuna?" Paul later told me this was a ritual he often performed to tell his friend, Djuna Barnes, the avant-garde writer of the 1920s, that he was keeping an eye out for her welfare.

At one time Paul Engle was poetry's bright young hope on the American scene, the subject of a full-page paean in the *New York Times Book Review* for his *American Song*. Understandably, he had this tribute framed and displayed on a stand in his Iowa City living room when I visited there decades after the publication. He continued to write throughout his life but never topped his *New York Times* triumph.

He was a true poet, however, and the proof lies in an incident he told me about. He was in the hospital for some disorder and during the night all the lights in his section were dimmed or turned out. This became a problem when the genesis of a poem entered his mind. Unwilling to lose it, he roamed about and finally found a refrigerator in a kitchen area. Pen in hand, he opened the door of the fridge and got enough light to write out his nocturnal inspiration.

While his poetry brought acclaim, it also fueled his spiraling career as administrator of the University of Iowa literary workshops. "You know why I like writers?" he asked me one day. "I like them because they're so interesting." He certainly was. To my delight, he told me we were distant relatives, confirming the matter by showing where his Cedar Rapids origin intertwined with my Amana nexus.

So, my Amana background helped cement this neat friendship. It also got me into Harvard, as I learned during my first semester there when I received a message to report to the admissions dean. The summons had me a bit worried but this genial man immediately put me at my ease by recalling the day my application crossed his desk. "I saw that you were from the Amana Colonies," he related. "I'm from the Mennonite community near Iowa City. I immediately thought it would be nice to get a young man from Amana into Harvard." And so he did, though I'm sure my grades had to play their role.

I truly cannot recall anything in my post-Harvard life that the college, excellent though it is, helped me with. Wait, I will make one exception. In my first semester the roommate assigned to me was Richard Robbins, a most genial Quaker lad whose ready laugh and broad cultural interests captivated me. I was deeply disappointed when some personal situation led to his leaving school for several years. Our friendship did not falter, however. We kept in touch and visited from time to time while he pursued a library career and entered a happy marriage with a jolly girl named June whom he had introduced me to. Easily the best thing that came to me from my Harvard years was Rick Robbins — yes, Rick, and not Richard. When Richard Nixon came upon the scene, Richard Robbins was appalled and forfeited his given name, becoming Rick.

For some years Rick was a prison librarian in the Providence area. He thrived on the experience. "You know who's in those prison cells?" he volunteered one day. Puzzled, I waited for him to go on. "You and me," he said. "It can happen to anyone — and often does. People take a wrong step, usually out of desperation, I suppose — 'and that made all the difference,' to quote Robert Frost's *The Road Not Taken*."

I'll get back to Frost in a minute but I want to say one more thing about Harvard. It is unquestionably a fine school but if I had a choice today between going there, where after all I earned a B.A. cum laude, and Maharishi University of Management, I would not hesitate for a second — I would choose MUM.

Why? Because Harvard is career oriented, and very good at that, but it does not address what I now view as the sine qua non of education; it does not give the student knowledge of the Self. "Know Thyself" was inscribed over the entrance to the Greek oracle at Delphi, where I once visited. By making Transcendental Meditation the basis of its education system, MUM addresses this lofty goal. How I would love to replay my college years, spending them at Maharishi University and thus sparing my physiology the beating I gave it early on when I could have been culturing my mind and body each day and raising my state of consciousness. Today, students at MUM receive regular brain integration report cards that show them what progress they are making.

And now back to Robert Frost, who wrote about those two roads diverging in a wood and then choosing "the one less traveled by." Every day, it seems to me, we are faced with variants of this dilemma, forcing us to choose one or the other. Quite often, when my intuition is nodding, I simply toss three pennies and let them decide what I should do, best two out of three. If the coins come up in a way that disappoints me, it shows that I did have a favored road after all. Then I toss the coins again. Dear little coins. Eventually they come up as I want them to!

26. Adventures with Anthony Quinn

Cioran, the Romanian-born philosopher quite popular in France in recent times, weighed in on this matter. "When you have to choose between two alternatives, one thing is certain," he was wont to say. Everyone of course asked what that thing was. "Whatever choice you make," he would reply, "you'll regret it, wishing you had picked the other!" Percipient fellow.

Actor Anthony Quinn once told me the very same thing when I was working with him on his autobiography. This would have been 1970, when I was living in West Hollywood, where I had just written *The Moguls*, about the heads of the film studios. The phone rang in my little studio and a chirrupy voice said, "This is Marjory Looney and I'm calling on behalf of Anthony Quinn. He wants to know if you'd like to work with him on his book, his life story. If so, he'd like to get together with you."

We met a few days later in his bungalow on the lot of Universal Pictures where he was filming a television series in which he played the mayor of a small town. He was tall, easily 6′ 2″, but also big-boned and hearty in manner, so that he seemed larger. His familiar voice was resonant, pleasing. Pauline Kael once wrote that watching Quinn on screen was like warming cold hands in front of a roaring fire.

Speaking of Pauline, I was introduced to her in 1965 when she was film critic at the *New Yorker*. The publisher of my first book, *The Child Stars*, had sent her a copy and she told me she had found it "compulsively readable," which of course pleased me. But let's get back to Quinn.

Talking to him was stimulating. He gave me all his attention and had a dozen stories at the ready. When I said that I had written a book about Greta Garbo he told me he was once at the Metropolitan

Museum of Art admiring a painting when he felt someone watching with him. He turned and gazed into Garbo's startlingly blue eyes. "Painted by a man," she said somewhat sadly. "No landscapes by ladies. Maybe I become a painter." "You should," he said, "and start with landscapes!"

And so it went with Quinn and myself. Two hours later he said, "Well, I'm ready to go if you are." I had passed the audition. "Mind you," he added, "I wrote something more than a decade ago and gave it to Little, Brown & Company. One editor after another has worked on it, unsuccessfully. Your task will be to succeed where they failed."

"Can I see what you've written?" I asked, whereupon he handed me a folder containing well over a thousand pages!

These took all my attention for the next few days. More even than writing, I love editing. I quickly saw what needed to be done and called him. We would get together for a week or so, he said, while he was between episodes at Universal. We would drive off to Death Valley, not that far away, and work there in an ambience familiar to him, a refuge in the past and a good place to get things done without disruptions.

The following afternoon I met Marjory Looney, who came to pick me up at the apartment complex where I lived. She was pleasantly English, perhaps in her late 20s, with curly dark brown hair, nice features, and a teasing smile. We picked Quinn up at his house on Alpine Drive and headed for the Furness Creek Inn, one of the few places where one could stay at this time in Death Valley. The rooms were modest, but the food was very good, and the glories of Death Valley surrounded us, negating the name.

We quickly settled into a routine, with work in the mornings, excursions in the afternoon, a pleasant dinner at the hotel around 6 o'clock, followed by another work session until 9 pm, "and so to bed," as diarist Samuel Pepys was wont to say.

I found it great fun to get up early and go for a walk around the palm-shaded grounds, picking fresh dates to whet my appetite for the breakfast that awaited. Once we started to tackle the manuscript, it was like rolling downhill. I went through page after page crossing out repetitive words, lines, and even whole paragraphs, with the keen-eyed author leaning over to see what I was doing.

Sensing that I was dealing with a half-Mexican macho personality, I wondered how long he would take my controlled but still savage slaughter of so many of his words. Page after page spun by, and each time a dozen had accumulated he passed them on to Marjory, who scurried off to type the revisions while I pursued my task, with Tony ever more attentive but still silent.

By the third day I had made a good deal of headway, and was actually speeding up, when I was startled to hear him shout, "Wait!" Here comes the macho moment of truth, I said to myself. I put down my pen and he took up his. Slowly, meticulously, he crossed out a repetition I had missed! I laughed and applauded with sincere admiration. By observing me at work he had become a good editor in a very short time. I might add that it's easier to edit someone else's work than your own, which may be too close to your heart. Fortunately he had not looked at his manuscript for several years, so he could be quite objective.

In a week we pruned over half the pages, but that left the other half to finish. It was some months before he had another break at his film studio. Then once again we piled into a rented car and returned to the Furness Creek Inn. This time we had an additional passenger, a lanky blond girl in her 20s, quite sweet, I thought, simple and straightforward. Work on the manuscript continued at a good pace and I began to get a feel for some of the trappings that go with success in the film world.

At the inn, everyone on staff was of course respectful and deferential to Quinn, though not unduly so, since Hollywood icons stopped by with some regularity. In the restaurant a three-piece combo provided background melodies for dining and here our every entrance was met with a robust rendition of the theme from Tony's great screen success, "Zorba the Greek." The musicians and diners always looked our way, hoping he would break into the rousing dance he had performed in the film. He never did.

And then one evening, as the little band was playing a soft Spanish serenade, he suddenly jumped up, walked over to a table some distance away, and held out his hand to a pert, bright-eyed young brunette. The music instantly switched to the Zorba theme, with approval from all the diners, who were then treated to Quinn whirling his partner through the rousing dance. As the combo paused, he took the girl back to her table, left her there without a word, and returned to us amid enthusiastic applause.

Once it died down I said, "What was all that about? "Didn't you hear?" he asked. "She was telling everybody at her table that I didn't do that dance here because I hadn't done it in the film. She said it was a double who did it." Of course for the sensitive Quinn that would have been a provocation and a challenge, which he met with style. More than anything, I was amazed that he had heard that conversation at a table so far away. The rest of us had not. It showed me how observing he was and what a good listener, qualities that helped make him a great actor.

A few nights later we were again having our cocktails and dinner when a sloshed middle-aged man wandered over to our table and said, "Misher Quinn, my wife is jush crazy about you. She wantcha dance wishyou. Will you dance wishher?" Here's how Tony handled it. "Tell her thank you," he said, "but we're having a nice quiet dinner and we have a lot of things we need to discuss. Tell her thank you and enjoy your evening." He spoke so gently that the man couldn't break the spell. Mumbling softly to himself, he retreated.

Another day we decided to work away from our usual lobby area and took the car to nearby Zabriskie Point, where we had a stunning view, which, however, did not distract us from the manuscript. We were working at a good clip and felt away from it all when someone rapped at the window next to Tony. He dutifully rolled it down for a rather wild-eyed lady. "Are you Anthony Quinn?" she shouted. "Yes," he replied patiently. "You caught a big one."

"Can I have your autograph?" she said eagerly. "Yes, do you have a pen or pencil?" he asked. Alarmed, she uttered several versions of no. "Do you have a piece of paper?" he asked. The embarrassed negatives multiplied while I supplied pen and paper. Tony then fulfilled her desire for an autograph and bade her a polite but firm farewell.

A few days later we visited an enormous gaping hole where a comet had apparently crashed to earth years ago. The scene was dramatic and one could take a path to the bottom of the crater. When told it required an hour to do justice to the site, Marjory and I opted for a walk on the surface.

"We'll see you in an hour," said Tony as he and his blond companion started their descent. When I winked at Marjory, she said, "If you think he's going to grab her when they get down there, forget it. That's not his style at all. He always waits for the woman to make the first move."

Both on the drive from Los Angeles and also on our afternoon excursions Tony liked to stop for a glass of wine if a bar graced our route, the lower keyed the better. I never saw him take a drink but an occasional glass of wine was on his agenda. In this case, Marjory and I elected to stay in the car and chat while he went inside. Half an hour later, with evening setting in, we noticed a big commotion outside, with scores of people, mostly black men and women, swarming around Tony, who was making a rather triumphant exit. Everyone was buoyant, happy. He, too, seemed in good spirits. Once back in the car he told us that he had really enjoyed himself.

"I couldn't believe it," he said. "They've seen all my pictures."

"And I imagine *Zorba* was their favorite," said I.

"No! *The Magus!*" he replied with enthusiasm, citing one of his lesser-known flicks, in which he was cast against type.

The moon came up as we drove along and I reported this to Tony at the wheel. He asked excitedly whether it was over his right shoulder or the left. When I said the right, he exulted, "That means good luck!" Or did I tell him it was over the left? Anyhow, it was definitely one or the other!

27. Anthony Quinn Redux

During this second visit to Death Valley there was one last, far more dramatic adventure. As I said, each afternoon Quinn rewarded himself and the rest of us with an excursion. We went to Scotty's Castle, with its links to local history. We gazed at a bleak area said to be the lowest elevation in the United States, some 280 feet below sea level. We explored other local sites, including a park with a high scenic ridge. There, Quinn and the blond girl took off in one direction, leaving Marjory and me to take a different route.

We agreed to meet at a designated spot, but when the rendezvous hour came there was no sign of Quinn and his partner. Marjory and I thereupon headed in the direction they had gone, all the while calling out "Tony!" as loudly as we could. No answer. Further on there was still no response. We became concerned because daylight was fading and the park was about to close.

Still deeper into the high-ridged valley we walked, calling in vain, until finally we heard a distant reply. We hurried toward it and gradually it became louder. Finally, we were just below the return calls. Quinn and his partner were high up on the ridge and could not get down.

"Why not?" I shouted.

"This is very treacherous ground," he replied. "Every time we move, we loosen boulders that could fall on us. Go for help! Try to find some park rangers. Somebody must be patrolling the place."

Marjory and I hurried toward the parking area and noticed that the few cars still in sight were all on their way out. Just as we started to feel panicky we saw a park ranger's car approaching. We hailed it and explained the situation. The rangers instantly signaled for colleagues to come with a pulley, ropes, and other tools needed to get people down from the precipitous height.

More time passed while we waited but eventually reinforcements arrived. Though they knew how to get up the steep cliff even in the complete darkness that had now settled on the park, getting down at night was too precarious on foot. The pulley was the only way to go. Up a narrow path they went to the top of the ridge. Painstakingly they anchored the pulley in solid rock and one by one everyone was lowered down, a time-consuming process.

I remember that when Tony descended he asked his rescuers not to alert the media to the events of the evening. "I don't want them to think Tony Quinn can't hack it," he explained. They reassured him and were true to their word.

By now it was midnight and much colder than the daytime temperature. Yet, somehow a mood of euphoria overtook us all. Quinn asked the rangers to call the inn and have them prepare steak dinners with baked potatoes and drinks for everyone involved. The copious cocktails and wine cinched a convivial end for this trying excursion. Summing it up very neatly was Marjory Looney. "Being around Mr. Quinn is not always easy," she told me, "but you can be sure of one thing — it's never dull!"

A day or two later something happened that proved her point. I was working as usual with Quinn, making great strides, when he paused to tell me of the period in his life when he was co-starring on Broadway with Laurence Olivier in the play *Becket*. At the same time, huge billboards on Times Square were heralding two films he had recently completed.

"A happy time for you, I'm sure," I suggested.

"Not at all," he said pensively. "Believe it or not, it was one of the worst periods of my life. I was depressed, almost suicidal. I didn't feel my life had any purpose or meaning. I remember I was at some gathering where I was being honored, no less. I just couldn't sit there one minute longer. I made some lame excuse and got outside. I actually ran down Fifth Avenue and into Central Park, where I threw myself on the ground and started sobbing."

I waited before asking, "And then what happened?"

"I had a spiritual experience," he said.

He did not wish to elaborate but years later, when I met him after starting to practice Transcendental Meditation, I suggested he might want to try it.

"I already meditate," he said."

I thought he might mean that he did some form of concentration or contemplation, thinking nice thoughts and so on. "I mean a specific technique," I told him. I mean using a special sound called a mantra to meditate."

"I have a special sound," he said quite simply.

"Who gave it to you?" I asked.

"God," he replied.

Well, that was hard to top. I took advantage of the revelation and used it to open his autobiography, an appetizer for the main course.

We had a touchy episode during this second trip to Death Valley. Those thousand pages of the manuscript took Tony — as I now called him at his behest — only to the age of 21 or so, although forward flashes dealt with later years, such as the one I suggested to open the book. Tony was half Mexican and half Irish. His mother was a simple, good-hearted woman from Mexico, still alive at this time, and elderly, the recipient of monthly checks from Tony that he later learned she gave away to family and friends. His father was a fiery Irishman, whom Tony adored. He died, alas, at an early age. Most of the book told of Tony's early years going up and down the West Coast trying to earn a living — picking grapes, entering marathon dance contests spawned by the Great Depression, making a stab at a boxing career, whatever brought in a few bucks.

As an adolescent he radiated a boyish charm, attracting the likes of Mae West, who was ready to cast him in a somewhat ambiguous role in her life if not on stage; Aimee Semple McPherson, a charismatic evangelist at whose temple young Quinn served as an usher; and Frank Lloyd Wright, who met Tony via an architectural venue and recommended that he have surgeons remove a speech impediment, an operation that took place and left him with his vibrant vocal tone. Teenage Quinn also met the great novelist Thomas Wolfe at a Hollywood Boulevard bookstore. The two became quite good friends and Tony once accompanied the writer on a memorable weekend trip to Philadelphia, an episode Tony was reserving for volume two of his memoirs.

Oh, yes, I was telling you about an episode of our joint editing job. Tony wrote virtually everything in the book himself save for a few transitions and the opening I devised. I also helped with the title, which he called, after much searching for alternates, "The Original Sin." He was rather vague at first about the exact meaning but I eventually got him to define original sin as "the inability to give love or receive love unconditionally." If I had it to do over again, I would fight even harder against that title, which makes a good point but does not really encapsulate the content of the book.

As for that touchy point, here it comes. Tony loved to write. When I say that, I mean both the mental process and the physical act of putting words on paper. He liked to write by hand on long yellow legal pads. In his *Who's Who* sketch, as I recall, he sometimes put "writer" ahead of "actor." He was also a fine artist, had a top gallery showing him, and made quite a bundle selling his paintings.

While we were at Death Valley various Hollywood acquaintances stopped by to say hello to him. Never once did he introduce me. I'm sure he was afraid that if he did they might assume that I, being an author, was ghost writing his book. He did promise the publisher that he would give me a page of acknowledgement. However, Little, Brown editor Harry Sions later told me that whenever he asked him for the promised paragraph, Tony found a way to put him off.

Still further on, when he went to the major publishing convention of the year to plug his book, the first question put to him by a reporter was, "Who wrote your autobiography, Mr. Quinn?" He did not hesitate for a moment. "That's supposed to be a curve, right?' he snapped. "I wrote it, every fucking word!" It was basically true. I did the touching up — a lot of touching up!

And as he saw all the little changes I was making, it made him want to do something himself to give the book more bounce. One day he proudly handed me a dozen pages of dialogue to replace a stream of prose narrative. I saluted the idea and his enterprise but on reading the passage carefully I saw that it was forced, flat, and less interesting than what we had already done.

When we discussed the matter, he defended his effort tenaciously and finally I blurted out. "You can do better, Tony. This is lazy writing." Well, I had chosen the worst buzzword in the dictionary for a sensitive man. He grasped the pages under discussion, stood very erect, and paused.

"I've waited 20 years to get this book into print," he said briskly, "and I can wait 20 more!" He might have used a coarse adjective with "book," but I'll give him the benefit of the doubt. You, clever one, may guess what it may have been. What's that? Aiee! I never thought I'd hear that word slip through your lips!

In any event, the next morning he did not show up for our work session. I went to the desk and asked them to call and tell him I was ready to go. Some minutes later, to my relief, he showed up.

"I'm glad you called," he said.

That was it. We never talked about it again. We finished the job at hand, turning a thousand pages into a little over three hundred. We met once more in New York when he got the page proofs. For a week we went over all the editor's queries. When the book came out it was well received and went into a dozen or more foreign editions. Of course none of them carried a page acknowledging my help. I didn't care that much. The fee I received was perhaps too modest but I didn't mind that either. Quinn was a blast. That was the real reward.

He spoke of doing a second volume and said he would be in touch. He also explained something that I thought was gracious.

"We've gotten to know each other really well," he summed up. "It's natural to think the friendship will continue. What happens though when I start another project is simple. The past has to be left behind. Everything goes into the new picture. So you may not hear from me for quite a while. That's just the way it has to be."

About a year later he did call and asked me to meet him at the Hotel Bel-Air in Beverly Hills for a drink and to catch up. In those pleasant surroundings we had a neat relaxed hour or two even though other people were milling about. He once told me he had 60 people on his payroll — relatives, friends, and business liaisons. Some interrupted our little session and the phone rang quite often. Amidst the low-level hubbub he said again that he wanted to get together on a second book. We would go extensively into his later life, most notably the film career and his amours, plus more about his personal philosophy of life.

We parted on a good note and shortly thereafter I received the only letter I ever had from him. Prior to our meeting I had started Transcendental Meditation. In the letter he said, "I have never seen such a transformation in a human being." I had certainly grown calmer and less judgmental. When I think back on it, in those years that I spent in New York and Hollywood the usual language was raw and rough.

I know one day during a political discussion with Tony I called Henry Kissinger an asshole for his Cambodia policy. I caught myself and apologized. "It's your favorite word," he said. I did use it a lot. On some days just about everybody seemed to me to be an asshole. We were all into cocktails in that era and drink loosened the tongue and lowered the standards of speech.

Marjory Looney told me that while we were working together Quinn often did an imitation of me. When we ordered pre-dinner cocktails I would habitually wait until I was the last one to order.

Then, just as the waiter was about to leave, I would catch his eye and say rather softly, almost surreptitiously, "Make that a double." Marjory said Tony had me down to a tee.

I once asked her who his closest friends were. She said there were two, director Stanley Kramer and putdown comic Don Rickles. Puzzled by the latter? So was I.

"What do those two talk about?" I asked.

"Philosophy and spiritual matters," she said. "Both of them are great readers."

Tony once told me he had five thousand books in his library, all of which he had read. He knew Thomas Wolfe personally, as I mentioned, and loved his writing, along with that of F. Scott Fitzgerald and Ernest Hemingway. He greatly admired Hemingway, especially his espousal of "grace under pressure." Though it never came to fruition, he worked for years on a one-man show that he was hoping to do in the manner of Hal Holbrook on Mark Twain. He said he had several chances to meet Hemingway but turned them down because he was afraid he would be disappointed. And well he might have been. The burly author could be … challenging.

28. Thoughts on a Writing Career

I had one more major adventure with Anthony Quinn. Should I tell you now, or some other time? All right, some other time. I hope I remember. One last thing though. I believe Tony really had a strong spiritual side that he didn't show to everyone. He was looking for answers to the riddle of life and he was definitely interested in the various paths to enlightenment. His first wife, who was Cecil B. DeMille's adopted daughter, explored Eastern religions in her later years. He was always bumping into that side of life.

Mark Twain, when he was writing about these matters, said, "When I speak of the laws of nature, I mean God." Modern physics has discovered the ultimate state of things through mathematical formulations and given it a name, which at the moment I cannot recall. If you can, you're a smart cookie.

I do recall though that Albert Einstein said, "I do not believe God plays dice with the universe." To this, another great physicist, Niels Bohr, replied, "Who is Albert Einstein to tell God what to do!" The Western method for arriving at final truth is objective, while the Eastern method is subjective. Which would you rather have, mental knowledge of the transcendental state or the experience itself?

A New Yorker cartoon comes to mind where two monks are seated in the lotus position on a mountain overlooking a vast horizon. "Nothing happens next," the caption quotes the one monk. "This is it."

For those who have experienced that numinous state — and I have encountered quite a few at special courses of Transcendental Meditation — there is clear evidence when one has arrived. All I spoke to agreed that the bliss is intense, though never uncomfortable. Life is easy, serene. There are no mistakes. Desires are spontaneously fulfilled.

I often recall that gathering called "A Taste of Utopia" back in 1983, when over eight thousand volunteers rushed to Iowa to practice their Transcendental Meditation technique as a group to bring more harmony to the world. At a talk he gave in Maharishi University's Golden Dome of Pure Knowledge, named after the ancient Vedic sage Patanjali, Maharishi spoke the words that changed the course of my life — "Why waste your life on little, little things?"

For a year or two I didn't respond to that query. I continued my routine as it had been. But every time I undertook some new obligation, some fresh activity, those words kept beating in my brain — "Why waste your life on such little, little things?" Finally, I gave up. I committed myself to a long advanced meditation course and in one form or another I have continued in that vein to the present day. Mind you, I still live in the workaday world and I do pursue useful goals from time to time, but only when they mesh with my spiritual quest.

There, I've spilled the proverbial beans! A while back I told you about these two main strands of my life and I also said that by reading on you'd see which one came to predominate. Yes, I gently favor the spiritual, but not to the detriment of the practical. Quite the contrary, since once the inner life starts to blossom it illumines the outer as well in a win-win situation, as Maharishi explained. Yes, dear, I've no doubt said all this before, but it's well worth repeating, yes?

I'm reminded of a conversation I once had with my good friend Allan Vincent. Allan was a very handsome young man when he starred on Broadway in Noel Coward's first hit play, *The Vortex.* Although his acting career was respectable, he was more addicted to the written word. His screenwriting efforts reached their apogee in the award-winning film *Johnny Belinda,* starring Jane Wyman.

After I became a resident of West Hollywood in the 1960s someone introduced me to Allan, who was by then past middle age and largely retired. He was a great reader and together we made frequent trips to local libraries, returning bundles of books and combing the stacks for more.

Once, after reading a heap of biographies, we started analyzing these lives, what made them tick, or not tick, and what made them worthwhile. I broached to Allan my theory that each life was designed to teach a lesson, or maybe a series of lessons. "So you believe we're in school," said Allan. "If so, I'm probably getting poor grades." "Me, too," I concurred, "but I hope to keep from flunking."

Now, decades later, I seem to have confirmed my views about the school of life. We can't make much progress if we make mistakes and keep repeating them. Enlightenment means shedding more light on things so that we can view them with greater insight, succeed in each undertaking, and bring benefit to the surroundings and ourselves.

Have you read much Somerset Maugham? He went to India at one point and spent several months with sage Ramana Maharshi, whose spiritual teachings were in vogue at the time. On his return home he used this India experience in his popular novel, *The Razor's Edge,* which has twice been transferred to the screen. The first starred Tyrone Power, while Bill Murray took the lead role in the more recent version.

In my youthful years I loved Maugham's stories, many set in the exotic lands encompassed by the vast British Empire, on which the sun never set. Not by any stretch the greatest stylist in the world, Maugham had the storyteller's gift for swiftly making characters come alive, for creating memorable scenes.

When I started out as a writer I wanted to emulate him. I fantasized traveling around the world, hanging out in public squares and pubs with locals or travelers, hearing their stories, and putting them down on paper. In later years I tried hard to bring it off. I wrote about a dozen novels, some of which came close to being accepted, but "close" is definitely not enough for an author.

It took me years of futile endeavor to realize I didn't have the true storyteller's gift or the first-rate novelist's command of technique. I could put in hours of labor and come up with something respectable — I did finally publish one slender science fantasy — but I didn't have the essential ingredients in sufficient degree. I also saw that I didn't have a really driving passion for writing fiction. While I had always thought it would be, well, kind of romantic and easy, it wasn't at all. Blank pages of white paper, yellow legal pads, romantic? Not a bit.

During my period as a New York editor I was eager to write a novel but each time I came up with an idea my friend Marguerite Young would shoot it down and urge me to stay with editing. However, when one day I proposed a book on the child stars of Hollywood she swiftly changed gears and shouted, "Do it!" How right she was to endorse this non-fiction idea with a built-in readership. Leaving my editorial job, I made my way to the New York Public Library and started a book about the child stars right then and there, using that facility's vast resources. Six months later the deed was done.

At a social gathering, a friend asked me the name of my agent. Amazed to hear I didn't have one, she wrote out a list of 10 for my consideration. The first was very high powered, she said, but probably would not have much time for me as a new author. The second possibility was a relatively new girl in town, Lynn Nesbit, with the esteemed Sterling Lord Agency. I chose Lynn, who read the manuscript over the weekend and sold it the following week to the first editor she approached, Ellis Amburn at Coward-McCann. I had done my writing job quite well, but what luck! Sterling himself took over my account a bit later and sold the string of books that followed, including *Three Sisters in Black,* recipient of a special Edgar (Allan Poe) Award from the Mystery Writers of America. I must say he was very genial and even-tempered, never ruffled by urgent calls from his roster of celebrity authors. Whenever I called with a question, he was available, unhurried, and helpful. I had that nice feeling of being in good hands.

Sometimes I think I have a fair enough "upper story," and sometimes I think it leaves much to be desired. Alan Pryce-Jones, that genial writer and bon vivant, once told me my mind was original and that I should think of taking up writing. His comment influenced me, but let me explain something about the mind that alternately puzzles and intrigues me.

When a minor dilemma presents itself, my thoughts often do a fandango of repetition that annoys and bores me, especially if the issue is some friend's real or imagined slight. Usually I don't want to think about this drivel at all. I hate to find fault in others. My mind, however, is like a dog with a chewed-up bone, getting no satisfaction any more but unwilling to let go — such a waste of time, but what to do? Let me know, resourceful one, what you do in these silly circumstances.

Shall I tell you now about that last adventure I had with Anthony Quinn? Nay, it will have to wait for a few days because I'm about to go out of town for a project. You will next hear from me right after my little trip.

29. A Final Episode with Quinn

I've returned in good spirits, and I'm pleased to see you looking so well. When I got back to my computer this morning, a friend had left me this message with a quote from that comic genius Oscar Wilde. Here's what he says: "A man's face is his autobiography. A woman's face is her work of fiction." Are you laughing, dear? So am I.

I'm sure you know James Thurber's beguiling sketch, "The Secret Life of Walter Mitty." Walter Mitty's mind spins fantasies of daring and courage that are quite harmless. Mine spins fantasies about what others are thinking and in the process manages to find shortcomings and faults. I hereby disown such thoughts. Since the thoughts come involuntarily, I guess I will have to disown them again and again. Well, it will give me something innocuous to do!

Now may be a good time to tell you about my last meeting with Anthony Quinn. It took place in 1979 when he called and asked if I was ready to work with him on the second volume of his autobiography. I told him I was raring to go, but the circumstances turned out to be most unusual. We were to meet in Libya in the middle of the Sahara Desert!

He was going to make a film called *Lion in the Desert,* the true story of a Bedouin schoolteacher who had fought to drive Mussolini's Italian troops out of Libya during the period between the two world wars. Although Libya and the United States were hardly on cordial terms at this time, I was not concerned about the dangers involved, since Tony was my sponsor. As for combining his film role with our labors on volume two of his memoir, that would work out. Much of the time he would not be needed on the set, leaving ample hours for us to do our job.

First, I was to go to London because it would be easier to get a visa for Libya from there than from the United States. Though I audaciously asked for $1,000 a week for my services, Tony forcefully talked me down to $600. Since I was doing only freelance work at the time, and making peanuts, that figure looked good to me. I had sought the larger amount because I felt underpaid for my work on *The Original Sin* — a mere two grand in total.

In London, a room had been reserved for me at the venerable Hyde Park Hotel, where Tony liked to stay; it was also the preferred London spa of Winston Churchill. Tony was already in Libya, so I had a lovely paid holiday while waiting for the Libyan Embassy to grant my visa, a simple procedure that took almost three weeks, due no doubt to the strained US-Libya relations. I had most of my meals in the hotel dining room and visited with some old friends who were living in London. I also got tickets from the hotel broker for many of the shows in town, including a festive closing night of the London production of *A Chorus Line* and an equally fine performance of the hottest ticket in town, Andrew Lloyd Webber's *Evita*.

When I finally got the official ok, I flew to Libya's capital city of Tripoli. I was met by a courier who drove me to the spot where Tony's film was being shot smack in the middle of the Sahara Desert. Quite a number of buildings had been constructed to cover the film crew's needs and when I asked for Mr. Quinn I was directed to a large recreation hall.

Entering, I saw a maelstrom of people scurrying about. I was wondering what to do next when a curious thing happened. Within the surge of activity my gaze was somehow drawn to a far corner of the hall. There I spied Tony standing quite still but looking in my direction. He definitely had that curious magnetism that the great stars share.

After greeting me, he immediately drove me in a rented Jeep to an isolated desert spot with not a house or even a bush in sight, only fresh clean sand in every direction. For a long while we stood and gazed at the silent, majestic Sahara, falling under its spell.

Actually, that was probably the best experience I had during the ensuing six weeks. After the Sahara, Tony took me to a pleasant villa I was to share with his new companion/secretary, a young Italian-American girl. It was situated in a very small town close to the film company's compound. The girl was bright and simpatico but I found I was not to enjoy very much of her company. Although she remained in our villa during the day, as night approached she sauntered off to a somewhat larger residence occupied by Tony.

I soon told him I did not feel comfortable in a strange house alone, especially at night, and he quickly arranged a room for me with the rest of the production company. Since the Libyan government was supportive of the film, it had built the huge recreation center with its restaurant, billiard room, and movie theatre, as well as a sizable outdoor swimming pool. The dormitories were likewise constructed by the government, which would reclaim them for army use once the picture was completed.

On the first day of filming Quinn returned from that day's desert location in a foul mood. When I asked what was wrong, he was silent and annoyed by something that had occurred. The next day he seemed a little less grumpy and I repeated my question.

"If you have to know," he said, still frosty, "I'm the Bedouin hero of the film, who's on horseback a good deal of the time. In my very first scene I fell off the goddamn horse! What a way to start a film!"

Things improved thereafter. His old friend, Greek actress Irene Pappas, was on hand, a tall, stately figure addicted to wearing lovely loose capes appropriate to the climate. It was their seventh film together. I often chatted with her and one day she asked me a question — "Why do you think Tony is writing this book?" "I think it's his way of getting to know himself better," I volunteered. "He wants to know what his life means, if it has a meaning." Pappas shook her head. "What do you think?" I asked. "What motivates him?" "Money," she replied gleefully, rubbing her thumb and fingers together in a symbolic gesture.

The budget for the film, I learned, was pegged at $25 million, but soon went to $35 million, allowing for high-priced stars like Oliver Reed, John Gielgud, Rod Steiger, and Raf Vallone to play cameo roles. Libya's ruler, Col. Muammar Qadaffi, was several times rumored to be coming for a visit to the set but never showed up. Tony's Italian-born second wife, who had over the years given birth to their three boys, arrived for a brief visit and departed.

The days passed pleasantly. Tony gave me a batch of books to read, saying they might be valuable later when we started work. Other than possibly reflecting aspects of his current state of mind, I could find little relevance in them. One day while we were chatting in his villa he went to a shelf and took down a sheaf of manuscript pages, riffled through them, and murmured, "There's some really good stuff here." "Maybe I should look at it?" I suggested. "Not yet," he replied.

So I continued my life of leisure, sitting by the pool, reading, or taking long walks in the surrounding desert countryside. One day I wandered rather far afield and was suddenly confronted by a sign saying I was trespassing on government property. For a moment I felt alarmed. With a quicker pace than usual I returned to the film compound.

Another day I joined one of the British actors on a visit to the shops of the nearby hamlet where I had spent but a single night. We also inspected some of the villas like the one I had occupied. My companion told me that I, or anyone else for that matter, could live in one of them free for two years, with only one condition. "What's that?" I asked. "You would have to convert to the Muslim faith," he replied. Well, I had given up my apartment in Hollywood when leaving for the Sahara, so I was free to shop around for a home, but this was clearly not it. When several female members of the film cast went shopping in Bermuda shorts rather than full-length skirts, villagers gave them a very cold shoulder, along with a sprinkling of stones.

As the weeks went by, some four or five by now, there were periodic meetings with Tony, who continued to heap praises on the manuscript resting on one of his shelves, but every effort I made to gain access to it was firmly rebuffed. Naturally I wondered why. Was he afraid I wouldn't appreciate the work he had already done? Had he really begun writing? Increasingly I asked myself what was going on?

I have a theory, and here it is. I believe Tony wanted me there for two reasons. If time did in fact permit, we could put it to use working on his book. However, the arrival of his wife Yolanda was perhaps another reason. Yolanda might not be unhappy to see Tony with an attractive new secretary if the girl was sharing a house with a nice young fellow — myself! When I failed to fall in line with this arrangement, much of my value to Quinn may have disappeared. Why should he pay me $600 a week for doing nothing on his as yet non-existent work if no other purpose was served?

In any event, a week or two after Yolanda departed he called me in and said, "We're not getting anything done, Norman. You're not doing anything. I think maybe we'd better call it a day — for now." Indeed, we were not getting anything done! And true, I was not doing anything. But who was to blame?

If Tony was ready to dispense with me, at this stage I was quite ready to move on. Sitting at a swimming pool in the middle of the Sahara Desert and reading a random selection of books was good for a few weeks, but in the long run a state of ennui set in.

We had a good haggle over finances and this time Tony gave in and agreed to pay me for the time spent in London. "I think when you look back on this, you'll find it was a good experience," he summed things up. I have, indeed, dined out many an evening on my Libyan adventure.

Lion in the Desert came out in 1981 and slowly began to pay off its investment. The elaborate location compound, the production crew of five hundred people, and scenes featuring up to ten thousand extras, mainly from the Libyan army, had kept costs spiraling.

Historical accuracy was clearly a target of the producers. Here they were aided by Benito Mussolini, who had had cameras film much of his Libyan campaign. The film's director even hired the barber who had once shaved Mussolini to shave Rod Steiger, who played Il Duce in the production.

As a rider to my adventure in Libya, let me recount a story Tony told me there on the sands of the Sahara about the great Italian director Federico Fellini. Did you ever see his film *La Strada*? Quinn plays a touring strong man who performs his feats in little towns aided by his adoring but sadly neglected sidekick, touchingly played by Giulietta Massina, Fellini's wife.

One night Fellini set up cameras in a small Italian village and shot one particular scene over and over again. All the villagers were out watching even though the hour slowly crept past midnight and still Fellini could not get past the troublesome scene. Wearily the actors went through their paces again and yet again until, finally, the scene went so well that the sleepy townspeople applauded. A tired Quinn was greatly relieved until he heard Fellini call for take 23.

"But Federico," he pleaded, "they loved it, they applauded."

"They're not supposed to," Fellini snapped. "They're not supposed to like you. Take 23!"

Once more the actors took their places and eventually Fellini got what he wanted. The critics were later unanimous in their praise of this cinematic gem by a gifted, intuitive, and painstaking artist.

The performer Quinn most admired, he told me, was Marlon Brando. "What about Laurence Olivier?" I inquired. He shook his head. "As an actor, maybe," he replied. "As a human being, give me Marlon Brando." He appeared on screen with Brando in *Viva Zapata* and also played Stanley Kowalski, Brando's signature role in *A Streetcar Named Desire,* on Broadway. People often forget Quinn's impressive legitimate theatre career, which included not only *Streetcar* and his co-starring role with Olivier in *Becket,* but also a long Broadway run in a stage musical that echoed the film *Zorba.*

Here's a final anecdote about the latter. Quinn asked me one day if I had ever gotten into another person's skin, even for a moment.

Not really, I admitted. At times I've tried to put myself into someone else's shoes, but the results were never noteworthy. "I can't play a role unless the pill goes down," he countered. "I have to become the person I'm playing."

Usually, he told me, weeks of research and rehearsal did the job. Not so with Zorba. As the first day's shooting drew near he was still in the dark about his character; the pill had not gone down. All night before the film's start he agonized, tossing and turning, getting up and plopping back on the bed, frustrated and fearful of the dawn. Finally, lying still, he sensed that for the first time in his career he would have to miss a film's starting date. Defeated but also resigned, he gave up and let go.

"And then," he told me, "the miracle manifested, as it had so many times in my career. The pill went down. I knew, absolutely knew, who Zorba was, what kind of man he was. God, it's exciting when it happens. In the morning I was one of the first on the set. I couldn't wait for things to begin. Alan Bates, you'll recall, was in the film with me. I saw him arrive. I ran over to this reserved Englishman and threw my arms around him. I kissed him on the mouth, only it was Zorba, this character with a lust for life, who kissed him. I was Zorba!"

30. Now about Free Will, Determinism

One nice dividend from my association with Tony came along some years after *The Original Sin* came out. Little, Brown & Co. asked me to repeat its success by doing a similar job with the autobiography of Rex Harrison. The plan, once approved, would be for me to go to his villa in Portofino on the Italian Riviera where we would work together for an estimated six months. I would be paid a hefty sum quickly agreed upon.

Accordingly I flew to London, where I was met by Harrison's agent and put up for the night at a club in Berkeley Square where those nightingales, at least in the song, allegedly sang — actually, they have apparently not been heard for over a century.

The following day the agent took me to Harrison's lair, a rather posh setup in a stately row of Georgian houses. Inside, Harrison, tall and very elegant, graciously shook my hand and guided me around a pack of noisy, panting pugs to a comfortable chair. He offered me a glass of sherry that I accepted while he abstained. We chatted amiably about this and that, the agent always attentive, and then we got down to business.

"I hear you worked with Anthony Quinn on his book," he began.

"Yes," I replied. "It was easy. We pruned down his thousand pages of manuscript and turned them into a very readable three hundred."

"Ah, here the task will be quite the opposite," he said. "I have fifty pages that will have to be turned into a very readable three hundred."

"No problem," I said cheerily, sipping my sherry. "We'll flesh it out with theatrical anecdotes."

His smiling face became cloudy.

"I loathe theatrical anecdotes!" he said forcefully, underlining "loathe" and making it sound quite odious.

At that moment I had a strong feeling the book might be a tough sell. However, we visited some more and I left on a good note. The agent was buoyant.

"I think you'll get the assignment," he said. "He liked you. We'll know in the morning.

I slept fitfully because of something that came out during the session. The Portofino aspect of the project was off. Harrison had taken on a Pirandello play with which he was going to tour the eastern part of the United States, the likes of Scranton and Pittsburgh. The change in plans disturbed me. I saw myself in dreary hotel rooms in towns that were a far cry from the Italian Riviera. Despite the strong financial terms I was wondering how I could get out of the whole business.

In the morning my dilemma resolved itself. The agent called, said he was mystified, but for some reason Harrison had chosen another editor, one he had interviewed several days earlier, ironically a former employee of Little, Brown now employed by another publisher. He was relieved when he saw that I was elated.

I called Little, Brown, told them what had transpired, and predicted that the book would have at best a modest success. This proved to be the case. The agent later confided that he thought Harrison passed on me because he had just married a 22-year-old beauty and probably didn't want a young man of my age around the house. The man he chose for the job was much older.

I almost forgot. My Libyan adventure did have a final, truly dramatic moment. On the day of my departure one of the film group's officials told me to bring my passport to his office so he could give the OK for my leaving. When I got there he looked at the passport and said, "Where's the stamp for your arrival in Libya?" I had no idea what he was talking about and told him so. When he appeared agitated, I quickly picked up on it. "Will this delay my departure?" I asked, now intensely eager to say goodbye. "You may never leave this country!" he said solemnly.

This was more than I could handle. I told him I was going to my room and could be reached there. I was so rattled that I lay down on my bed and immediately fell asleep. It was my way of coping. I was awakened several hours later by a courier who returned my passport.

"Everything's in order, sir," he reported. I embraced him with a thank you so hearty it almost bowled him over. Soon I was on my way to the airport and the flight back to London where my itinerary had me spending the night. When I embarked on British soil I threw all caution to the winds and dropped to my knees in thanksgiving. Yes, indeed, and don't think I didn't have a few drinks at the dear old Hyde Park Hotel, and a little bottle of wine with dinner, and a splash of brandy afterwards. I slept quite well, thank you.

Do you sleep well? Fitfully? Oh my, that can be a bummer. I've dealt with sleep problems all my life and I've learned some things valuable for myself and perhaps for you. The first thing to remember is that it's best to be as relaxed about the situation as possible. Apparently one can get 80 percent of the value of sleep simply by lying quietly in bed. Once you know that, you won't feel so panicky about getting to sleep or not getting to sleep. Next, find a comfortable position and try not to move around too much. When the body quiets down, the mind follows and also settles down. Some specialists say every hour before 10 pm is worth as much as two after 10, so it's wise to get to bed early. A final nice thing to know is that once you're settled in bed it helps to take a deep breath. This, too, relaxes the body. Do it two or three times as you're settling down.

Using these ideas, or techniques, I rarely have trouble getting to sleep. I do, however, wake up often to go to the bathroom. This used to be once or twice a night but over the years it increased to three and four. Now I'm up six and seven times a night, a veritable nocturnal yo-yo. It seems to be congenital. My father got up a lot. I've been to literally dozens of doctors, including top specialists, and they see nothing wrong. They tell me to train myself to "go" less often. Ah, well, as someone said, "After 40, it's all maintenance, maintenance, maintenance."

In my 20s I weighed in at a hundred and eighty pounds. Since then I've been losing about a pound a year and now, at the age of eighty, I'm sixty pounds underweight at a hundred and twenty. At this rate I'll weigh one hundred ten pounds in 10 years, when I'm ninety, and only one hundred pounds a decade later when I'm one hundred. If I continue to lose a pound a year and somehow remain alive, I have one hundred years left to live, at the end of which I will not need to be buried or cremated because at that moment I will weigh nothing at all. So I have that smooth transition to look forward to and in my will I must scout out someone to whom I can leave the baby clothes I'll be wearing near the end.

Actually I've often thought it might be more pleasant to start life with old age and then grow younger and younger with the years. I even made notes for a novel I wanted to write with that theme until I learned that half a dozen writers had beat me to it, including F. Scott Fitzgerald, whose effort made it to the screen a while back.

Lest I forget, here's another illustration of how my mind sometimes brings forth thoughts not truly my own, thoughts I disavow. We now go back seventy years to a day of non-stop squabbling in the otherwise comfortable house I grew up in. Mom and Dad had a dandy row in the morning over breakfast, completely ignoring me. To show my disapproval I boycotted lunch with them and went to visit Aunt Marietta and Uncle A.T. They, alas, were having a lively wrangle of their own, largely ignoring me as a result, insult number two. Somehow I managed to hide my annoyance long enough to snack with them before going out to look for better company. When none was in sight I returned home to find Mom and Dad reconciled with each other but engaged in a brouhaha with Marietta and A.T.

By this time all the arguments and counter arguments had my young head reeling, and then to my amazement all four of them piled gaily into A.T.'s Studebaker to go heaven knows where, with everyone waving goodbye to me as I pondered my outcast state. I knew they'd have to drive down the long hill on which we lived to get to the next village. At the bottom they would have to cross Highway 6. In my mind's eye I saw them colliding head-on with a speeding car at the intersection, totaling all four hapless souls and thus ending all future arguments between them forever.

Now, mind you, I really loved them all. And yet this gruesome thought came to my mind and I've read enough Freud to know that at some level I must have desired their demise. Or did I? How does one handle this sort of roguish mind? I see no alternative but to disown these negative thoughts.

Whaddaya think? Am I the only person nutty enough to have this sort of internal drama going on largely against my own will? I once cornered the friend I consider the wisest counselor around on dilemmas like this. "How much free will do you think we really have?" I asked. "None," he replied without a moment's hesitation. That reply had considerable appeal for me. It absolved me in one swell foop of the heinous crimes of matricide and patricide, as well as unclecide and aunticide.

Even more satisfying, however, was the elaboration Maharishi offered a short while later when asked whether it was free will or determinism that ruled. "Both," he replied, "but it's best to think of it as free will." He went on to explain that clearly we have the freedom to choose whether to go to New York or Hong Kong. But once we opt for New York our freedom of choice has disappeared. It is now determined that the plane will fly to New York. All of life follows this formula. We are to some degree free and to some degree determined at each step of our way through life.

I recently saw a slim volume entitled *The Wit and Wisdom of Thomas Jefferson,* which showed that Jefferson, too, liked to explore philosophical quandaries. In the pages I read there was certainly some wisdom, but I could find little trace of wit. Recent biographies report that when Jefferson presided over a dinner table there was always lots of laughter. I believe it, but I have yet to see instances of anything he said that made people laugh. Maybe some of the guests made humorous remarks and he responded. He was apparently a good listener as well as a good talker.

Washington was also on the reflective side. Historians portray him as a most admirable, even a very great man, but hearty humor does not appear to have been one of his fortes, though he could get off a good barb now and then. It was a letter-writing age and letters were often used to dispense practical knowledge and guidance, especially from the older generation to the young. The Washington and Jefferson letters that survive bear this out.

You would expect that John Adams, a New England Puritan, might be overly serious. On the contrary, certainly not enough to preclude a good quip against himself, as when, nearing 90, he acknowledged that he was now at that venerable age "but still too fat to die." I like the picture of "His Rotundity," as he was sometimes called, having a good chuckle.

Adams by his very nature lends himself to humor, even when he's not trying. Take the wonderful night when he and Benjamin Franklin, on a diplomatic mission, had to share a room with a view, at least with a window. Franklin wanted the window open in order to get the fresh air. Adams wanted it closed so that he could be warm and comfortable. Just the thought of these two marvelous historical figures wrangling over the disposition of the window makes one smile.

31. Teaching French at Brearley School

That one word, window, brings to mind a long-ago day in New York. Just before landing with *Theatre Arts Magazine* I spent a year teaching French and German at Brearley, a top-rated Manhattan school that attracts young ladies from upper-class families with means.

While I was being hired, one of the teachers there gave me a bit of advice. Newcomers usually want the girls to like them, she said, and therefore they are very friendly and smile a lot. "Don't smile for the first few weeks," she cautioned. "Be serious and make them earn your friendship." I heard what she said but fell into the beginners trap. I smiled. The girls smiled back, and took that to mean they were free to do as they pleased.

Early on they tested me. When I called the class to order, most of them took their places, but one remained seated on a windowsill. "Cassy, please take your seat," I said. "Why?" she asked. "I can hear you over here." Well, she had me there. I went into a routine explanation and eventually persuaded her to join us, but the pattern was set. I had a distinct discipline problem and the girls got away with a lot. I'll have to admit they could be appealing at times and quite amusing.

One of them came to see me in my office and very kindly said there was no need for me to try so hard with her. "I'm not really interested in learning French," she explained. "I'm just a playgirl!" "Don't you want good grades?" I asked. "Don't you want to go to college?" "Nope," she replied. "Don't you look forward to going to France this summer with your parents to tone up your French?" "Nope," she repeated. "Well, what do you want to do?" I persisted. "I want to go to the beach with my boyfriend," she said with a playful laugh.

There were stretches when things went smoothly, but inevitably youthful high spirits took over. One day I came to class, sat down at my desk, and opened the top drawer as usual for my French grammar. I became aware that the girls were spellbound as a thick foggy mist billowed forth from the drawer. The little urchins had placed a slab of dry ice inside and naturally shrieked with delight at their own caper. What could I do but join them!

During a particularly trying period, pressure from the most difficult girl became so great that I asked for a meeting with school headmistress Jean Fair Mitchell. She listened attentively while I explained that this student was so routinely disruptive that I thought it might be better if she were dismissed. "I have only one question," Ms. Mitchell said in a kindly voice: "Could any other school do better than we do?" Instantly I was won over and withdrew my suggestion. Jean Fair Mitchell brought out the best in her faculty. My best was tested the very next day.

When I came to class I was happy to see everyone seated without my having to call them to order. I should have known something was afoot. There was indeed. Right in front of my desk, decorating the route to my chair, was a sizable heap of dog doodoo. The air was charged as the girls waited to see what would happen. I suspected one individual, a frequent trespasser, and spoke to her.

"If you are responsible for this, get a paper towel and take it away!" I commanded. "That won't be necessary," she cheerily replied. With that, she marched to punt position and gave the unsightly mess a swift kick. Riotous laughter ensued as the doodoo, made of rubber, bounced across the room. It was not easy to restore order that memorable day.

Have I told you about Maharishi's sense of humor? I may have given you an illustration or two. It was almost a constant and yet hard to describe. While he was quick to pun, his light-hearted take on things ranged widely.

One day during a lecture at Humboldt College he was describing some quite advanced states of consciousness when he paused to ask how many had had such experiences. Only a few raised their hands. Maharishi surveyed this modest response and said, "Almost everyone." At this, everyone laughed. As a result, he used the expression many times, making it his sure-fire signal for mirth.

Another day, when his lecture focused on the nature of love, he startled us by saying, "All love is directed toward the self." After allowing the silence to penetrate the hall he added, "Funnily enough." Peals of laughter pleased him so thoroughly that he repeated, "Funnily enough," eliciting the same response. His main thrust in this classic discourse was that we do things to satisfy ourselves, our little self. When we love someone, we do so because it makes us feel good to do so, he elaborated. When the person no longer pleases us, we tend to withdraw our love, and move on.

To illustrate this point, someone stood up and quoted Goethe, who said, "If I love you, what business is it of yours?" This elicited more jollity. Maharishi concluded by urging everyone to expand their consciousness, raising it from the small individual self to the infinite cosmic Self, making it a worthy object of love.

Many years ago, during a meditation course held at the foot of the Himalayas in Rishikesh, where Maharishi had an ashram, a participant found that he could not sleep and decided to go out for a walk, though it was the middle of the night. When he heard laughter coming from a second-floor terrace, he looked up and spied Maharishi and another sage sitting in the moonlight, their faces wreathed in smiles. Not one word was spoken. Silent shared mirth was the sole means of communication.

Something quite profound happened during the long gestation of this memoir and I have wanted to bring it up before. Somehow I could not do so until now. Maharishi Mahesh Yogi, great sage of the Shankaracharya tradition of Vedic masters, passed on. Even as I write this, I feel the power of that event. This was the unique spirit that taught me how to put together a life truly worth living. At every stage of my life, wisdom from his lectures comes back to guide me. His passing was a huge milestone for me.

A newspaper reporter once asked him when the world would come to recognize his true stature. His only reply was a serene smile. I have many friends who went to India for the final rites, which involved an elaborate cremation ritual that many who attended found at once moving and liberating, as though they too had cast off the weight and burden of their physical body.

At my present age the body does seem more cumbersome. In younger years I regularly "flew" in my dreams. I would have the desire to go up in the air, prime myself, and take off, feeling wonderfully light, seemingly weightless. I really loved it. Every couple of months this would occur. As the years went by it happened less and less. I rarely "flew" after the age of 60. Now I never have that exhilarating experience at all. The physiology must need a lot of flexibility in order to fly, even in a dream. Whatever is needed is what I no longer have.

Come to think of it, dear one, maybe I've got the next best thing. I've been having a recurrent dream where I'm on this spacious dirigible sailing toward Byzantium. For a while all is well, but I never get there and every flight is spoiled by my quandary as to whether in future I should pack winter garments or prepare for a more temperate clime. Your input in this matter will be greatly appreciated.

Somerset Maugham lived to a ripe old age, enjoying it less and less. At one of his last public appearances he was asked about the matter. "There are m-m-m-many advantages to b-b-b-being old," he stuttered, paused, and continued, "b-b-b-but at the m-m-m-moment I cannot think of any one of them!"

Tributes to Maharishi poured in from all over the world after his death. The media paid particular attention to the celebrities who had trekked to India in the 1960s to learn meditation from him, including remaining Beatles Paul McCartney and Ringo Starr, Mike Love of the Beach Boys, and singer/songwriter Donovan, all of whom were reverential in their praise. Deepak Chopra also weighed in, describing the time he spent with Maharishi as "the best days of my life."

My larkish nature is reminding me that if, long ago, Oprah had married Deepak Chopra, she would have become Oprah Chopra! I'm sure neither has lost sleep over this lost opportunity, this path not taken!

Is right now the best time of your life? No? Rats! But no need to fret. Something great may be lurking just around the corner.

I do think individuals with a creative bent have a certain advantage, don't you? To give you an example, I'm just now reading an excellent life of Henri Matisse. He suffered agonies for his art, but he had something substantial to show for it. At the end of one's life that must be a comfort.

In a television documentary on Maharishi he was once asked what he would most like to be remembered for. "Nothing," he replied. It was the perfect answer, I thought, totally free of the ego. Of course, he was a monk, and a monk's goal is to be free of desires, including the wish to be remembered. And dear Maharishi did leave behind a towering gift, some thirty thousand hours of videos encapsulating his knowledge and teaching.

This has been quite a colloquy. Are you getting a bit sleepy? So am I. Leadbelly's *Good Night, Irene* comes to mind. Do you know it? If I weren't so tired, I'd sing it for you. Let's just close our eyes for a few minutes and drift off to Snoozannaland.

32. Judy Garland Live, JFK Turns 50

How do you feel after that little catnap? Good. I'm glad. Yes, I feel fine, too, and all the better for your asking! To get back to aging and longevity, I recall something on the subject by Swami Yogananda, author of that seminal spiritual work, *Autobiography of a Yogi*. "Don't disclose your age," he counseled elderly followers. "If you do, people will expect less of you."

I've noticed that many of my friends are proud to have made it into the 80s or 90s. They don't want to hide it. I tend to agree with them. If people expect less of us, so be it. As I may have told you, my mom died at 96 and dad reached 92. Come to think of it, the two romances in my life that turned into lifelong friendships were both with lassies who lived well into their 90s.

I met Mary Lou Patterson in Los Angeles when I was 19. I saw her looking at a painting at the Los Angeles Museum of Art. She herself looked like a Madonna, and so what I said to her was, "Do you think American artists will ever paint Madonnas?" Some may well have done so ages ago, but I didn't know. I only wanted to gain her interest. Replying to my question, she laughed a wonderful throaty assent, and as we discoursed I realized I was speaking to a painter, and a very knowledgeable one.

The romantic phase of our relationship lasted about two years but we packed a lot into that interval. Mary Lou saw more of the beauty of the natural world than anyone I have ever known. On walks in the country she loved to share her bounteous sense impressions. On occasion I would plead with her to call an intermission lest my receptors be overloaded. Her paintings were often portraits of family members and friends, along with burgeoning commissions. She loved people and people gravitated to her buoyant spirit.

"She's the real thing, isn't she?" her mother said to me one day. I heartily agreed. She was the real thing herself and had a good eye for it in others. I'm grateful to her for turning me on to the Impressionist painters Bonnard and Vuillard, and in a parallel vein to the evocative orchestral works of Frederick Delius.

Our interlude of intimacy ended when I embarked on a European episode but our friendship continued for the rest of Mary Lou's long life via letters, the phone, and renewed personal acquaintance when for several decades I lived near her in Los Angeles and villages close by in California. In many cases, as people age their voice remains youthful and largely unchanged. So it was with her. I'm told that while everything grows old as we age, the ears are the last to go. Isn't that a comfort!

Mary Lou had a keen sense of the incongruous. One day she came back from a trip to her bank and said she had had a startling experience. She withdrew some money from her account and while making her way out she glanced at the bank's surveillance camera. She was stricken with pity for a little old lady with a severely stooped back and a wrinkled face. "Poor old thing," she murmured to herself — and then came a shock. She was looking at herself! More than anyone, she enjoyed this story at her own expense.

In one of our last phone conversations she told me she had left California and moved back to Springfield, Missouri, to be with her brother in their old family home. "Don't you miss California?" I asked. "Yes," she said, "but only during the day. In the evening, after dinner, I go to my room and close my eyes, and then every wonderful sight I could ever wish for from the past comes right into my head."

That was typical of Mary Lou. Whatever happened, she made a positive of it and turned it into art. Her mother, also an artist, had done the same thing. When I visited her one long-ago day she had just turned 93. She was bedridden but on the wall by her side she had painted a mural depicting a sunny beach scene — the ocean waves rolling in, children playing in the sand, surfers gliding gracefully in harmony with nature. She never spoke of missing anything.

My other lifetime courtship, with Rita Senf, a psychologist and editor by trade, also began as a romance and eased into genial camaraderie. Where Mary Lou was curvaceous and light of movement, Rita was tall and statuesque, yet equally graceful. Where Mary Lou's voice was refined, yet resonant, Rita's was soft and soothing, with a healing quality. Over these many decades I cannot recall Rita ever saying anything harsh or judgmental.

Neither of these wonderful ladies ever married, nor have I. Friendships, however, blossomed for both of them, as already noted. Most of the friends Rita introduced me to were males of the species. On the other hand, admirers of both genders could usually be found around Mary Lou. As for the ears of these two phenomena, I'd call it a draw — lovely little lobes.

Oh, yes, as I said, Rita had many male friends. She was the sort of person one could easily call on for a favor. I went with her one day to walk the dogs of a friend, after which we returned to his apartment. While Rita watered some plants, I pulled a chair over to a bookcase, chose a volume of poetry, and started reading. When she had finished her chores I headed for the door. "Wait, Norman," she said, "haven't you forgotten something?" I gave her a puzzled look. "Please put the chair back where you found it," she said. That was Rita, thoughtful at all times. I loved her for it.

While in this reminiscent mood, I will add a noteworthy occasion she brought about when we both lived in Manhattan. To thank me for several evenings out, she invited me to take her to the Forest Hills Tennis Stadium, where the much-adored Judy Garland was giving an outdoor concert. Though I was not a fanatic Judy groupie, I liked her songs well enough, and the tickets were already on hand, and so off we went.

Things began rather poorly. The concert was scheduled for 8 o'clock, but at 8:15 there was no Judy, nor at 8:30. Peter Allen, a young performer who was later to marry Judy's daughter, Liza Minnelli, was holding forth with a three-piece combo. They were doing very well but the crowd wanted Judy, and at 8:45 she was still absent. Now the multitude grew restive and started booing poor Peter when he came out for the third time.

And then something unexpected happened. The din in the stadium mysteriously subsided to near silence and everyone craned their necks to learn why. From one of the sports stadium's dugouts the tiny figure of Judy Garland came into view. As she walked slowly to the area of the stage, all eyes turned toward her and a swelling sound came out of that enormous crowd different from anything I had ever heard at an entertainment event, a stupendous sigh of relief and of love. This was followed by an almost fierce ovation as the entire multitude rose to its feet. Here she was at last and I was soon to learn what the excitement was all about.

Naturally her old standbys were on the program — *The Man That Got Away, The Trolley Song, San Francisco, Over the Rainbow,* and many more — interspersed with lively chatter from Judy, a born storyteller. I recalled that Mort Lindsey, the bandleader who had accompanied her on tour, said he had found her so funny that at the end of each day his jaw ached from laughing.

At Forest Hills, after each number, fans would shout out requests. This went on and on, until finally Judy pleaded, "I've sung them all!" At that point a voice rang out, "Judy, we love you!" The words galvanized the exhausted star, who whirled in the direction of her admirer and shouted back, pausing after each word, "Oh-no-I-love-you!"

To sum up, it was a love fest, Judy's powerful voice in splendid form, even the balmy weather cooperating to make it a night to remember. Later, when a CD set of all her recordings came out, the review I read found it remarkable that with all her originality she fully respected each song and never dismantled it to do her "thing," as was the case with some singers politely left unnamed.

As a grace note to the concert, here's an amusing story Judy liked to tell on herself dating back to a time when she wowed them at the Palladium in London. So pleased was she with her reception that she called her onetime Hollywood chum, Deanna Durbin, now married and living in nearby France, and recounted her triumph. No detail did she leave out of her breathless rendition, but finally, exhausted, she paused and waited for her reward. There was only a long silence, followed by these sober words from Deanna across the English Channel in France — "So you're still in that asshole business!" Judy could laugh heartily at the foibles of others but she never spared herself, one more reason her legion of fans adored her.

My second most memorable entertainer was Marlene Dietrich, whom I saw in Los Angeles late in her career when she did a one-woman show. Her entrance in a sexy flesh-colored outfit showed her famous legs to full advantage. Later, she sported a tux, bow tie, top hat, and slacks. Like Judy, she had the audience in thrall as she worked her magic through a run of her standbys, such as *Falling in Love Again, Where Have All the Flowers Gone? See What the Boys in the Backroom Will Have,* and even a surprisingly seductive *You're the Cream in my Coffee.*

Finally, I was one of the fortunate thousands who poured into Madison Square Garden in New York for President John F. Kennedy's forty-fifth Birthday Gala in 1962. A friend of mine had connections with the Catholic hierarchy and secured a prized ticket. Since he was an opera buff and only interested in the first half of the celebration, I lucked out. At intermission he made his exit, gave me his ticket stub, and left me to enjoy the historic occasion. Jack Benny, Maria Callas, Jimmy Durante and other stars were on hand, but it was Marilyn Monroe that seventeen thousand Kennedy supporters were waiting for.

The moment seemed to have arrived when host Peter Lawford announced her with expected hyperbole, but though the band played her entrance cue, she did not show. Another act took her place, after which our host again told us the one, the only, the fabulous Marilyn was ready. Only she was not, and another act came on. Anxiety and anticipation alternated until a distraught Peter Lawford, hearing the music cue for the third time, once more proclaimed the glories of Marilyn Monroe, and this time, to lusty acclaim, the charismatic star slithered across the stage in a Jean Louis gown that Adlai Stevenson later described as "skin and beads." She was well worth waiting for. She did not really sing *Happy Birthday* but breathed the familiar words toward the guest of honor, who shared in the applause. Later, her gown was sold at Christie's for a record $1.2 million.

There were other good moments at that New York event and for me the best was the inimitable Jimmy Durante wowing the crowd while facing in one direction, then personally swinging the piano around to give the other half of the Garden its share of showmanship by a master.

33. Groucho Marx, Tennessee Williams

After these positive reminiscences my mind seems to want to strike a balance. Brace yourself. One year in my childhood Amana home all the kids were told they would get a dime for every gopher they caught and killed in the surrounding fields where they were nibbling at the roots of growing grains. We all bought traps, set them in the fields, snared the innocent little gophers, and calmly whacked them to death, all for a dime apiece. It sounds so horrible, and was, and is. I think of it often, and ask forgiveness of the gophers. It never occurred to us at the time that it was a rotten way to earn money and yet I gain no solace by pleading ignorance.

Similarly, like kids all over I suppose, we ran after fireflies, those beautiful bits of blinking phosphorescence, put them in a jar, and marveled at them in their captivity. Sometimes we let them out at bedtime and sometimes we forgot all about it. Whenever I see youngsters doing this now I ask them how they would feel if some-one put them in a big glass jar. Of course they look at me with eyes that clearly indict me as a nut. I plead guilty to the charge. Yes, I know the bugs are very small, with only a speck of consciousness, but they are alive. One can't help stepping on living creatures but why go out of our way to hurt them!

Fireflies, I might add, are not really flies. Surprisingly, they are one of some two-hundred fifty thousand species of beetles, a num-ber that makes one wonder if God perhaps created the world not so much for man but for beetles. They use an enzyme to make their flashing "cold light." Scientists have spent years trying to unravel the secret of how they do it, without success, so far as I know. The female firefly uses her light blinker to attract males. One species, however, attracts males of another species and, instead of mating, eats them.

Writing about oneself can take one over treacherous terrain, as I've said. Do you keep a diary? Do you put in everything that happens to you, the good and the bad, the humorous and the baleful? If you do, my hat's off to you. *Chapeaux bas*, as the French say, which reminds me of a joke that had me laughing out loud. It's bilingual, which means I'll have to make sure and get it just right.

An American in Paris was asked to give the eulogy for a French friend who had died, and since he felt his French was up to it he spoke in that language, recounting what a wonderful man the deceased was, beloved of family and friends, having lived a long upstanding life and contributed richly to society. To conclude, he said with much feeling, *Capotes bas*, and doffed his hat as a token of respect. He had meant to say *Chapeaux bas*, or "Hats off," but instead he had said *Capotes bas*, which means "Condoms off" or "Lower your condoms." This created a mild sensation at the memorial service, climaxed by a distinguished gentleman in the back of the room who admiringly murmured, *Quelle delicatesse!*

Telling jokes is such a tricky business, isn't it? I just read something that Groucho Marx said about Lucille Ball — "Lucille Ball is only funny when she's got a script. Without a script, she's not funny." I do prefer the comics who make you smile on sight. Jack Benny immediately comes to mind, along with Groucho Marx and W. C. Fields.

I met Groucho in the 1960s through Erin Fleming, a pretty fledgling actress who was my West Hollywood neighbor at the time. Groucho, by then out of the public eye, hired her at $50 a week to answer his fan mail but ere long she was working at his house full-time and playing a key role in the revival of his career. She arranged for him to do one-night shows telling gags and singing old-time vaudeville songs. She was also responsible for putting him together with a pianist/composer friend, Marvin Hamlisch, who later had a huge success when *A Chorus Line* opened with his music.

Erin invited me to meet Groucho during this period and we chatted amiably. He was surprisingly small but brimming over with vitality, the ever-present cigar in place, a beret on his head, and the eyes twinkling with thoughts of incipient mayhem. "Since I'm her neighbor," I said, "I see Erin almost every day." "I wish I could say that," he replied with a Groucho leer for her benefit and mine. When the conversation touched on writers, I mentioned that while researching my book, *The Moguls,* I learned that Harry Cohn, head of Columbia Pictures, kept one long table at the studio restaurant reserved for the writers in his employ. "One long table?" mused Groucho. "Sounds like a Chinese restaurant." Puns dropped from his lips as lightly as raindrops from the sky.

Inevitably, as their relationship became public knowledge, the press wondered if Erin and Groucho were more than business acquaintances. Erin told me that she did sometimes spend the evening with Groucho and that occasionally he absent-mindedly called her by his last wife's name. She also said he wanted her to marry him. "But why would I?" she asked. "I've got a sugar daddy already. I don't need a second one." Groucho's family eventually tried to ease Erin out of the picture and complicated legal maneuvers ensued. Early on I urged her to keep a diary of her daily meetings with Groucho, capturing his unique gifts for posterity. I wonder if she ever did. At least to my knowledge, none has surfaced. But here's a neat anecdote about posterity.

When Harry Truman was in retirement after his White House years a major network came to Missouri to do a documentary on his current lifestyle. Bess Truman made a point of staying out of sight, but one afternoon the producer saw her hastily making an exit by a side door. "Mrs. Truman," he pleaded, "won't you come back and let us capture you for posterity?" Bess halted only for a moment. "I have no desire to be captured for posterity!" she replied, and firmly closed the door.

I said earlier that I would relate brief encounters with Groucho and with Tennessee Williams. I saw Tennessee several times at parties given by my friend Dan Blum, who knew countless celebrities as the editor of pictorial annuals on the theatre, screen, and dance, as I've indicated. At one of these I saw Tennessee greet Helen Hayes, who had just opened in *The Wisteria Trees*, a modernization of Chekhov's *The Cherry Orchard*. When he took her hand I noted that both were of modest height and both were clearly in a buoyant frame of mind. "Helen," he said, "you were mahvelous, the best thing I've seen since Laurette!"

Laurette was Laurette Taylor, the legendary star who overcame a bout with alcohol and made a sensational comeback in Tennessee's *The Glass Menagerie*. Some time later, at a New Year's Eve party, I recounted the party episode to actress Geraldine Page, who threw back her pretty head and shouted gleefully, "He says that to everyone!"

At the same party I asked Carol Channing, then the toast of the town while starring in *Hello, Dolly*, "What will you do when the show closes?" "Oh, honey," she gushed in her inimitable breathy delivery, "I'll take it on the road. You only get a show like this once in a lifetime!"

In the midst of the following summer, Dan invited me for a weekend at his house in Sag Harbor on Long Island. Actually, other guests were occupying the main house while I was relegated to a small guesthouse nearby. This suited me fine, however, since my annex was a storehouse of books relating to theatre and the arts. My delight at this cache became short lived when Dan suddenly pounded on my door.

"Norman, you'll have to move to the big house," he said, huffing and puffing, his portly frame quite out of control. "Shelley Winters is coming and bringing several friends. She's been here before and asked for your little hideaway."

It took me only a few minutes to pack my single bag and move. I was just in time to see Shelley arrive with her guests, who turned out to be two aspiring young actors. While working on my books and living in West Hollywood I had often spotted her around town at theatre hangouts. Just seeing her was an event. She usually wore a mink stole casually thrown over her graceful frame and an entourage of handsome young men invariably attended her. She was voluble, vibrant, an eyeful. I greatly admired her and looked forward to the rest of the weekend.

I was now living in a small attic room of Dan's main house and felt rather isolated. I turned on the radio at some point and heard startling news. Marilyn Monroe had just died! From reading Shelley's bestselling autobiography I recalled that she and Marilyn shared a Hollywood apartment at an early stage of their careers. I bounded down the stairs and rushed to the kitchen where I found Dan and an array of guests having a snack, Shelley among them.

"Have you heard the news?" I interrupted their chatter.

"What news?" asked Dan, not too pleased by my intrusion.

"Marilyn Monroe is dead!" I blurted out.

There was consternation on all sides. Everyone asked me questions. I gave what little information I had. Shelley got up hurriedly.

"Danny," she said. "Can I use your phone? I've got to call my psychiatrist."

Dan got up and guided her to the phone in his room. When he returned the only conversation was about this startling event. More than half an hour later, Shelley, looking distraught but controlled, returned to our gathering and uttered a sentence that I have recalled clearly ever since.

"My psychiatrist says that if I've learned something from this, Marilyn's death has not been in vain," she informed us.

I was startled by these words but everyone else took them in stride. It was, after all, the heyday of psychiatry and psychoanalysis. Shelley, moreover, was a star, and mass adulation tends to make even strong personalities insular. Take Katherine Hepburn, for example, who candidly called her autobiography *Me*. In my own experience, when Anthony Quinn and I got along so well on first acquaintance, his secretary felt prompted to issue a caveat. "Just remember one thing," she cautioned, "remember that Mr. Quinn is Number One."

In Sag Harbor on that sad day Shelley reminisced about her long friendship with Marilyn, to whom she obviously felt close. The talk about her untimely death went on for a while and then the daily routine of beach excursions and town chores fell back into place. The date was August 5, 1962. Marilyn was only 36.

Later in the year I invited Dan to Christmas dinner in the Edwardian Room of the Plaza Hotel, repaying his many invitations with this one special event. It turned out even better than expected. Once we were seated we found ourselves near a very trim looking Tennessee Williams, who was there with his fabled sister Rose, the inspiration for some of his finest female characters, notably the young daughter in *The Glass Menagerie*.

Seeing Dan engaged in long-distance conversation with Tennessee, the *maître d'* put our two small tables together so that we could be more comfortable. Dan and Tennessee talked shop while Rose and I listened and gobbled, me with gusto, she with delicacy. She wore a pale blue turban and looked quite regal. I had read of the trauma in her early emotional life, which led her mother to seek a frontal lobotomy for her, something considered acceptable at the time. At the table she did not initiate any talk but replied simply when from time to time I asked her a question just to be friendly.

Still on the subject of Tennessee, I'd like to tell you a story that grazed my funny bone when I read it in Gore Vidal's memoir, *Palimpsest*. At some point Gore pointed out to Tennessee that he had given his birth date as 1914 instead of 1911, slyly making himself out to be three years younger than he really was. Tennessee was quite ready for the challenge and delivered this riposte: "I do not choose to count as part of my life three years spent working in a shoe store."

When my elderly parents came to visit me in New York, several of my friends, Dan Blum among them, made a point of having them to dinner, which they greatly enjoyed. I gave a party for them at my place, too, and invited many prominent people whose names meant nothing to them. How different those two worlds were, the sophisticated lifestyle of New York and the far more sedate atmosphere of rural Iowa in which I began my years.

And yet, it seems to me that on close inspection the big city and the small town are often not that far apart. I'll give a lighthearted example. When Mom and Dad came to visit me in New York we dined one day at a sidewalk cafe in Greenwich Village. "Look, Mom, hippies!" said I. My wily old Mom cast a jaundiced eye on the colorful scene and then said disparagingly, "We have our own hippies in Iowa." Of course I must point out that she was German born, and the traditional joke about Germans is that it's hard to impress them since they've always seen bigger dwarfs!

34. Long-Ago Amana, Fairfield Now

Let's go back now to my birthplace in Iowa and share a sunset glimpse of that idyllic spot. I'll show you a sweeping view of all seven villages comprising the Amana Colonies, with rich forests and a river running between them. When I was a child, the hill was quite steep with a dirt road as the only access. Early automobiles, including our Model T Ford, and later our Model A, often got stuck in the mud and had to be pulled out by a tractor, the big event of the day. On one side of the road a procession of pines — most of them now gone — filed from the top of the hill to the bottom, where Highway 6, not yet heavily traveled, formed a border.

We had a three-word name, as I've mentioned, for my family's six-house hamlet — Upper South Amana. Down below across the highway lay Lower South Amana, and beyond that West Amana, High Amana, Middle Amana, Amana proper, the largest of the seven villages, and finally, East Amana, and Homestead, bought outright for its railroad terminal. As school kids, my young friends and I walked the long pine trail down the hill to our red brick schoolhouse in Lower South. The steep dirt road was leveled off in later years and gave way to modern cement, certainly more practical but much less picturesque.

In those serene days I often sat on the ground, just as we're doing now, and gazed at the panorama below, counting the automobiles snaking along the highway, fantasizing their romantic destinations in the great world just out of reach. President Hancher of the University of Iowa noted that the old traditions of Amana were in peril once Highway 6 came through with its intimations of the restless, tempting world beyond, "the outside," as we then called it.

Atop the hill, our wonderful old homestead was flanked by an open pasture where the cattle grazed quietly and glanced at us only momentarily as we wandered by. The woods behind the field were rich in blackberry and blueberry bushes, along with walnut and hickory nut trees, all of which we patronized in season. At some distance, a beautiful pine forest beckoned. We went there often to enjoy the cathedral-like silence, the sweet scent of pine in the air, and the cushiony bed of pine needles underfoot. After a hundred years or so, a virus took hold. The last time I went to Amana on a visit the stately pine forest was gone, gone with the wind.

Change rules the everyday world and the many phases of it. Do you know the poignant poem by A.E. Housman on this subject?

> Into my heart an air that kills
> From yon far country blows:
> What are those blue remembered hills,
> What spires, what farms are those?
> That is the land of lost content,
> I see it shining plain,
> The happy highways where I went
> And cannot come again.

Lucky children like myself, happy in their innocent adventures, are to some degree shielded from the full impact of the dramas and even tragedies that are taking place simultaneously during childhood. Though we had only six houses in Upper South, and Lower South had less than 50, looking back now I'm saddened by the dark days some of the residents lived through, the same sorrows reported on so fully in urban venues.

What's the answer to this dilemma? Can you guess what I'm going to say? Oh, my goodness, how perspicacious of you. Yes, I say meditation will work wonders by releasing stress from the nervous system and simultaneously raising consciousness. Other aids may be of some help but it's like putting a bandage on a sore rather than getting to the root of the problem.

And what better place is there to practice TM than right here in the fair field of Fairfield where two radiant golden domes — one for the ladies, another for men — are packed with meditators at both morning and afternoon sessions. Most of the seventy buildings Maharishi University inherited from a prior college have been replaced by "fortune creating" structures in the style of ancient Vedic architecture. All are therefore facing east to gain nourishment from the morning sun, and all meet other Vedic building precepts that structure life in harmony with natural law. Meals in the university cafeteria serve organic food and every effort is made throughout the campus to go "green" and sustainable.

This recitation means, of course, that the decision as to what to do with the rest of my life has just been made. I will stay here. In addition to what I have already said about the university, a paean to Fairfield itself seems to be in order.

This small town of less than ten thousand dwellers boasts a dozen good ethnic restaurants; even more cosmopolitan specialty shops catering to whatever is most attractive and health-giving; a new convention center with its 525-seat Stephen Sondheim Theatre for the best in culture and entertainment; a huge phalanx of fine artists who sponsor a monthly art walk patronized by several thousand visitors; an astrological observatory which is an exact replica from the ancient Vedic civilization; and a thriving business community that manages a mind-boggling percentage of the entire state's venture capital and presents job opportunities to many.

I'm saving the most important lure of all for last. While Fairfield has only a modest population, some three thousand of its residents practice TM. The presence of this huge extended family, like-minded in its twin goals of enlightenment for every individual along with peace, harmony, and prosperity for the world at large, is really incalculable. Sages speak of this communal bond as "satsang," which means keeping the company of like-minded seekers of truth in order to speed aspirants to their goal.

Mind you, I'm still not saying that I'm living the ideal life, free from mistakes and sorrows. I've been practicing TM for almost forty years but those years have taken their toll, and I'm still waging some of the old battles. Maybe next time around I'll reach the ultimate state of consciousness I long for. Meanwhile, though I do have an occasional rough patch to hoe, I seem to be happy most of the time, evolving at my own pace. And I see no reason why I can't take vacations to visit those tourist meccas I fantasize about. I should add that if I did get to heaven one day, no doubt after a time I'd start wondering if the denizens of the "hot place" were having a better time! Again I invoke Mark Twain. "Heaven for climate," he said. "Hades for good company."

Are we as a civilization evolving, as the theory of evolution suggests? The other day some columnist wrote that when you consider Darwin's theory, just look at the great leaders we had over two thousand years ago, giants like Julius Caesar and Alexander the Great, and compare them to the world's current crop. That alone, this sage said, puts paid to the Darwinian theory of evolution. He made his remarks, however, prior to the arrival on the scene of Barack Hussein Obama, whose stature is currently a work in progress.

I rather like those quizzes that ask prominent figures what their tastes are in reading, or what they'd like to change about themselves, or what they're proudest of in their own lives. I'm speaking of features like the "Proust Questionnaire" in *Vanity Fair,* which sometimes asks its subjects what form they'd choose in another birth.

Quite frankly, I don't want to reincarnate if I don't have to. I'd rather enter the state of Nirvana, or Enlightenment — which I've just decided to capitalize because it seems appropriate. But if I have to return, I'd opt to come back as an amalgam of Gore Vidal, for that scintillating mind, and Warren Beatty, for his knockout looks, when both were in their prime. I like what Elizabeth Taylor said about Warren — "On a scale of 1 to 10, Warren is a 15!"

By the way, I suppose you noticed the positive tone that came to me quite spontaneously when I spoke a while ago of my two ladyloves. Let me hasten to assure you that these were the best of my intimacies and not representative of the whole. My youth was the era of free love, a misnomer if ever there was one, and many of us were naive people puttering about in a playpen.

The main reason I'm reluctant to say much more is that I feel the rehashing of failed relationships would be quite painful. I think this might carry over to anyone on the receiving end. So you see, my dear, I'm sparing you! I'm always thinking of you, y'know.

Did I tell you that I once wrote an article for *New York* magazine called "The Y'Knows Have It?" I wanted to deplore the reliance on "y'know" and "I mean" in our culture. For a solid week I huddled by my TV and literally counted the number of times these two phrases popped up on late night talk shows hosted by Johnny Carson, Merv Griffin, and Dick Cavett. I thought Cavett's guests would make the least use of these phrases but it turned out there was little difference between the three shows. I seem to recall that one of Carson's guests managed a staccato triple "y'know" as a prelude to his next utterance. Edwin Newman, that kindly author and commentator on English usage, or misusage, kindly wrote a note commending me for my contribution to the cause.

Since I've spoken of them several times, you can gather that I've long been fascinated by America's founding fathers and the presidents. Over the years I've written perhaps a dozen Presidents Day quizzes, almost all for the Los Angeles Times Syndicate. What a marvelously motley crew I was dealing with, ranging from expressive Franklin Delano Roosevelt to "Silent Cal" Coolidge; from flyweight hundred-pound James Madison to sturdy heavyweights like Grover Cleveland and William Howard Taft, the latter weighing in at three hundred fifty pounds and splashing about in a seven-foot bathtub at the White house; from models of probity like George Washington to Warren Harding, who, in the words of Alice Roosevelt, eldest daughter of "Teddy," "put the White House closet to uses no one had ever thought of before."

The highest office is certainly a vast reservoir of amusing trivia. George Washington wrote copious letters, no less than nineteen thousand of which survive, and in this avalanche how often did the father of his country mention his mother, well known as a feisty female? The answer is twice. Let me add that he loved to dance and could hold the floor for hours at a stretch. He was also a natty dresser, his clothes supplied by the best London tailors. We all know that Thomas Jefferson wrote the Declaration of Independence and made the historic Louisiana Purchase, but did you know that he invented the swivel chair, and the Lazy Susan, and brought a new novelty, ice cream, home to America from France?

Millard Fillmore became president when Zachary Taylor died in office in July 1850, the first chief executive to succumb while Congress was in session, with much resultant media coverage. Today, Fillmore is one of the least known of our presidents, the very name Millard a seeming portent of obscurity. I should add that Zachary Taylor was a second cousin of another president, James Madison. Dwight Eisenhower's mother was a Jehovah's Witness. Gerald Ford was the only man to become vice president and president without being elected to either office. Oh, and we must not forget James Garfield, our 20th president, who certainly had the best parlor trick of any White House occupant — he could write, simultaneously, Latin with one hand and Greek with the other. This has never been topped.

I have several friends who met one or another of our presidents, sometimes shaking their hands, but I have personally encountered only presidential contenders. During his first campaign for the highest office I worked for Adlai Stevenson. When he came to his Manhattan headquarters all of us hailed that genial, gifted man. I also worked in Bobby Kennedy's New York senatorial campaign, carrying a placard on one occasion and almost touching him. Note that he almost made it to the presidency and I almost touched him. So you see I came quite close.

35. California and Hummingbirds

I forgot to tell you the other day that if I had to come back for another lifetime, I might opt to be a hummingbird, such an amazing creature, weighing less than a dime, yet capable of traversing the Gulf of Mexico without stopping for gas — i.e. nectar. If I were destined to return as an insect I would have resort to the order of Lepidoptera and become a butterfly. What an adventure it would be to flutter from North America all the way down to Mexico and rendezvous there with millions of other Monarchs. Of course humans reincarnate as humans, but isn't it fun to play around?

When I lived in California in the 1970s, in beautiful Laguna Beach, I had a confrontation with a hummingbird at my marvelous little house on Catalina Street with a distant ocean view on one side and a back porch overlooking Bluebird Canyon on the other. Even without feeders I saw the hummers all over the place doing their skydiving courtship maneuvers or patronizing the wild and potted flowers offered up by the canyon and its denizens.

Once I put up feeders with artificial red nectar a steady stream of hummers visited my porch. Not a day went by when I didn't have a feast for the eyes while they had a feast for their dainty tummies, though I later learned that store-bought food was really not good for them. In any event, all went well as half a dozen varieties of these welcome guests graced my patio, all at once in some cases.

And then disaster struck. My regulars were wonderful looking, perfectly formed, and radiantly colored. To join them, however, came the homeliest hummingbird I have ever seen. The feathers, so delicate on the others, were ruffled and looked like they might have been damaged in some bird brawl. While the varied colors of the other hummers changed with each shift of the sun and wind, the invader's constant shade was a dull gray monotone. To top it all off, this renegade would not make friends with the regulars. No, indeed, he disturbed them at their spigots and drove them off!

Clearly, something had to be done. I tried several stratagems. Whenever I saw the trespasser, I took a flyswatter in hand, not intending to strike but merely to warn, to indicate a degree of unwelcome. It was no use. On seeing me the sharp-eyed snoop would opt for another feeder, or find some beauty, presumably of the opposite sex, to molest.

Bit by bit I noted fewer hummers coming to my feeders. Having started with six, I reduced the number to three in order to make swifter sallies in these patio frays. Nothing worked, however, and I opted for a more drastic move. I took down all the feeders for a week. My thinking was that my regulars, along with their nemesis, would take me off their daily itinerary, leaving me to start afresh — hopefully without you know who.

I missed my hummer friends dreadfully during that week. In fact, without them I felt like a pariah. With happy anticipation, therefore, I put all six feeders back in place. I placed a chair at a discreet distance so that I could observe my new crop of visitors and hear the melodious whirr of little wings.

Not one hummer arrived. Though I sat for the better part of an hour, book in hand, I was too distracted by my mission to pay it much heed. I tried again in the afternoon, with the same result. Nary a hummer. The following day I visited the patio regularly and once again its empty feeders stared back at me. At the end of the week, nothing had changed. My house was obviously under quarantine.

See what an exacting person I can be! Instead of accepting the world of the hummingbirds in all its rich and varied complexity I had tried to impose my judgmental human standards on it. The hummers must have a way of communicating over great distances. Clearly, word had gone out that some heel on Catalina Street was mistreating one of their members. The hummingbird council of elders had settled the matter by crossing my address off their itinerary.

Birds and animals can be very sensitive. My friend Jim Rollins had a lovely Siamese cat named Raja that was graceful, sweet-tempered, and very bright. One day he brought home a pretty goldfinch he had caught unawares and laid it proudly at Jim's feet, as cats are wont to do. Instead of appreciating this gift, Jim, saddened by the bird's demise, scolded Raja forcefully, "Bad kitty, bad kitty, never do that again!" Well, Raja stopped eating. After all, he was only doing what cats do instinctively, which is hunt birds, among other things. Jim pleaded and asked forgiveness, as one would do with a human friend. He tried everything, plying his pet with goodies from the table. It was no use. Raja would not eat, wasted away, and died.

Curious, isn't it, how the mind flits from pillar to post. I was thinking how Jim was impotent in that situation, and then my mind turned to another thought I've long had about this delicate area of life. My theory is that men who are impotent often become abusive of their wives for that very reason. They want to be manly, to be fulfilled by their sexual prowess, but for whatever reason, they can't if they haven't got it. Men handle this dilemma in different ways. Some are lucky enough to have wives who are happy to be left alone, but men with unstable egos may not want to shoulder the blame for conjugal abstinence. They will put the onus on the woman, declaring her to be so unappealing as to be undesirable. This will leave her so confused that she may indeed start feeling she must be at fault.

Then a second step follows. The man starts abusing her, a slap here, a verbal assault there. This escalation produces something unexpected. The man, having brought into play his sadistic tendencies, gets excited—and begins to embrace his lady, much to her relief. There may even be declarations of love and appeals for forgiveness from the man for his earlier brutality. This seems to be a happy ending, but it only sets the stage for an unfortunate cycle. With time the sessions may get rougher. Who knows how many individuals have dabs of masochism and/or sadism lurking in the basement or attic of their nature. So there's the dilemma.

Well, what do you think? There must be some underlying reason, probably unconscious, for some men doing deplorable things that they periodically regret and then repeat. What did you say, dear? Some men are just assholes? Naughty, naughty! You just employed what used to be my verbal standby until I cleaned up my act. No, I'm not offended by your using it, you or anyone else. Don't feel I'm being holier than thou.

For myself though, I no longer like to use it. What's that? I mean the word, dear, not the actual organ. The word just doesn't resonate as favorably as it once did. I'd rather use a less caustic term.

Shall we go to a movie, my little chickadee? Good. However, I have a confession to make. I have never been a great moviegoer. Yes, I know I wrote all those books, but they were more about screen personalities than about the art of film. I am not an expert in that category. I must also tell you that very often I walk out on films quite early on. I can tell in about 10 or 20 minutes whether I'm going to like something.

My preference is for something beautiful to look at and with a plot that offers charm or inspiration. Dark subjects or suspense are not for me. As a young kid I used to get frightened very easily in that dark and musty movie theatre in Marengo, Iowa, the closest cinema to our home. Even Laurel and Hardy, when they got into trouble, made me uncomfortable. I thought what was happening on screen was real, that they were in dire straits. I was always bewildered when I heard those around me laughing.

I was really naïve and of course part of that came from my background in Amana. Everything was so well ordered that there didn't seem to be much need to think for oneself. When I was in my late teens I had a startling revelation. I was suddenly aware that I had just had a thought of my own, not something I was repeating from someone else. At that moment I sensed that a whole new world beckoned and off I went to join the navy and seek adventure on the high seas. I only got as far as Great Lakes Naval Training Station but I did begin a new life away from home.

What did you say, my pet? Oh, yes, the movie. There's nothing really good playing, is there? Let's do it some other time. I'll go home and read. I'm in the midst of this fine biography of Henri Matisse. I'll loan it to you when I'm finished with it, if you're interested. You're not? Why not? He's considered one of the great painters of the 20th century. You don't know enough about painting? Neither do I. That's one of the reasons I'm reading the book.

All my adult years I have dutifully visited museums in this country and abroad. I've spent many hours gazing at masters from the past, like Raphael, Titian, and Rembrandt, along with moderns like Cezanne, Picasso, and Matisse. I've enjoyed myself, as much for the sociable museum ambiance as for the art itself.

However, I have never had a peak experience looking at a painting, a moment when, as the Richard Rodgers song goes, "My heart stood still." I suppose you know that Rodgers was driving along in Paris with friends one day when a near collision occurred and a lady in the car said with a shiver, "My heart stood still!" Rodgers filed away the idea and wrote the song years later.

Getting back to painting, one sometimes hears of connoisseurs who have "the eye." At a glance they pick up every aspect of a work's greatness, easily spotting a masterpiece. Thomas Hoving, former director of the Metropolitan Museum of Art, is said to have had this rare gift.

Matisse was able to surround himself with an entire family of art lovers, a wife and three bright children, all of whom lived basically for his work, reveling in the intimate aspects of each masterpiece he created.

Over the years of my writing career I have had some fine moments, and on occasion I have also made a stab at painting. Stab seems to be the right word. I purchased a palette and some paints, but the results gave no hint of a latent talent.

Music, too, eluded me when it came time to practice at the piano. My teacher tried gamely to make my fingers glide over the keys and produce harmonious sounds. It was not to be. I also tried the guitar. The guitar made it clear that I had better leave it alone.

36. Housman, Poe, Frost, and Emily

And, oh my, what an obstacle course confronted me when it came to sports. I was ready to go out for baseball but my brother's wicked fastball beaned me, leaving me ball shy and consequently error prone. I had high hopes for tennis but the net stood in the way of any success. Golf balls were too small for my swing to connect with anything but green turf. In college I tried boxing and did quite well with a nice little guy who had short arms, but faced with equal limbs I was soundly thrashed.

My last effort was to go out for the cross-country track team. My feeling was that if I could not succeed at sports involving skill, surely I had a chance at the simple art of running. I liked to run. I liked the country, so why not go for it? Well, I did, and found it extremely trying. Where a light sprint was fun, slogging over the miles was no treat, especially with coach alongside in his new car shouting for all to hear, "Lift your legs, champ, lift your legs!"

I stuck it out, however, and made it into a climactic race through a new territory within the city park. As usual, I started to fall behind early. It was not long before the twists and turns of the route put me so far in the rear that I lost all track of my buddies. With no one else in sight, I was relieved to see a small sandpit and a pretty little girl playing in it. "Which way did they go?" I called out. She seemed to understand and pointed in a direction that I readily followed.

Soon I was pleased to see the end of the route ahead. To my utter amazement I was the only runner in view. I drew myself up proudly as I crossed the finish line to applause from the smallish crowd that usually attended our events. Our coach, however, did not rush to greet me and a moment later I could see why. My buddies came blazing down the trail and a much louder burst of applause rent the air. It seems I had innocently clipped one mile off the two-mile race.

Oh, well, as someone wisely said, "You win a few, you lose a few." I thought it was bad form for our cross-country mentor not to give me a sports letter at the end of the semester, especially when every one else got one. It would have cost him nothing at all and it would have made my day. I rue the loss of that letter. Do you know A. E. Housman's touching little poem using the word "rue"?

> With rue my heart is laden
> For golden friends I had,
> For many a rose-lipt maiden
> And many a lightfoot lad.
>
> By brooks too broad for leaping,
> The lightfoot boys are laid;
> The rose-lipt girls are sleeping
> In fields where roses fade.

Robert Frost also used "rue" in a neat little poem.

> The way a crow
> Shook down on me
> The dust of snow
> From a hemlock tree
>
> Has given my heart
> A change of mood
> And saved some part
> Of a day I had rued.

Frost said an interesting thing. He said many interesting things but here I refer to his statement that if you can tell which of two rhyming lines came first, then it was probably not a good rhyme. If you couldn't tell, that was the real thing, good poetry. Let's experiment with this precept in Frost's little poem.

In the first two lines I cannot tell which of the two rhyming words came first—so far, so good. However, in the last two lines, I feel strongly that the line ending in "mood" came first, and then Frost had to come up with a rhyme for that, which turned out to be "rued." "Rued" seems strained to me, not a natural expression. So that confirms Frost's precept in his own poem. I wonder if he would agree.

Do you? You couldn't tell which rhyme came first and like the poem just as it is? Well, Frost would be happy about that. However, I have thought of alternative closing lines. Would you like to hear them? You can't wait, eh? Well, here they are.

> Has given my heart
> A gentle tuck
> And saved a day
> That had run amok.

How do you like that, dear? You still like Frost's version better? Well, so do I. I was just kidding around. I rue the moment I started this!

While I've never transcended over a painting, I've had some profound moments reading poetry. As usual, Emily Dickinson comes to mind. I always think of her as Emily. There's only one extant photo of her. It shows a small sensitive face. A friend once saw me walking down the hall and swore that he thought I was Emily. I do not look at all like her, but there you are. Here's another tidbit for your consideration. Emily and Walt Whitman are the two American poets that musicians most often put to music.

For the French, however, the foremost American bard is Edgar Allan Poe, who exerted considerable influence on Gallic literati like Charles Baudelaire, an early translator and advocate. Now here's a good trivia question. Which of his own poems did Poe admire most? No, it was not *The Raven*, his best-known work. My guess is that guessing will get us nowhere, so I'll tell you the answer. It was *Eureka*. Never heard of it? Most people fall into that category. One of his last works, *Eureka* is a 50-page prose poem in which Poe expresses his view of the material and spiritual universe in elevated terms. He asked his publisher to disseminate this work widely, but only the French seem to have become meaningfully aware of it.

As for Emily, here are some of the poems that I've read many times. As you know, she never stooped to the cliché use of names for her works — i.e. "I am now going to read you *Bumblebees* by Bertrand Bottomley" — so corny. Instead, everyone uses her first lines. In my edition of the complete works I put asterisks next to *Because I Could Not Stop for Death; My Life Had Stood a Loaded Gun; I'm Nobody, Who Are You?; These Are the Days When Birds Come Back; I Heard a Fly Buzz When I Died;* and *There Came a Day at Summer's Full,* to name just a few. Emily is sometimes called a tragic poet because she often dealt with death, but that is a misinterpretation. She was always searching for the light and she often found it. "Life is ecstasy," she summed things up. "The mere sense of living is joy enough."

Oh, I forgot her powerful *Wild Nights, Wild Nights.* Yes, demure Emily had her tempestuous nights, though we will never know if romantic fantasies or spiritual ecstasy made them so. The latter, I would guess.

How could she write 1,750 poems without anyone suspecting such bounty! Well, look at the great Franz Schubert, now considered by many critics to be in the very highest pantheon of composers. Franz had his legendary Schubertiades, evenings where he played the piano and friends joined him for music, especially songs, he had composed. During his lifetime, however, he heard almost none of his superb chamber works or symphonies performed in public. How could he go on with so little acclaim? He was put on earth simply to compose, he told a friend.

I also think with compassion of Beethoven. There is that indelible image of him at the premiere of his *Ninth Symphony,* where the finale, the stirring *Ode to Joy,* was greeted by thunderous applause, which he, however, could not hear because he was deaf. A colleague had to turn the great man around so he could see the audience clapping.

In like manner, my heart goes out to Vivaldi, composer of *The Four Seasons* and a flood of other fine works. The redheaded priest was acclaimed for decades but ended his life in poverty. I may already have told you that Georges Bizet died only two months after critics turned a deaf ear to his superb opera *Carmen*.

37. Utopias and *The Ramayana*

Here's another trivia question for you. Over all the long stretch of years in which music has been around, which was the richest of all? It makes you think, doesn't it? I'll give you the answer supplied by radio program host Bill McLaughlin. He chose 1685. Naturally you ask why? Well, in that single year three great composers were born — Johann Sebastian Bach, Georg Friedrich Handel, only a few miles away, and Domenico Scarlatti, a bit further south. Many years produced rich musical harvests, of course, but how could they compete with the lifetime output of these three giants?

I listen to music, mostly classical, for at least an hour every day. That's the background for my great interest in composers. Here are a few upbeat notes. Robert Schumann was an unusually kind soul, welcoming 20-year-old Brahms as the successor to Beethoven. Brahms was equally gracious to struggling young Anton Dvorak, sponsoring him and guiding him to his own music publisher. Brahms was also one of the best friends of Johann Strauss Jr. and loved his lilting waltzes. Once, asked for his autograph, he wrote out a few notes of a Strauss waltz and underneath added, "Unfortunately not by — Johannes Brahms."

Back we go for a second to Schumann, who became a composer by accident. He wanted to be a concert pianist, felt his fingers were too short, and used a mechanical contrivance to lengthen them. Instead, it caused permanent damage and made him turn to composing, a sunny turn of events for him and the world.

Turning to France, we encounter Camille Saint-Saëns, who was truly versatile — a major composer, skilled pianist, and prolific author. Hector Berlioz, no slouch himself, paid him a deft compliment. "The only thing he lacks," he said, "is inexperience." Curiously, on his deathbed, Saint-Saëns requested that all copies of his *Carnival of the Animals* be destroyed. That wish was not granted and it remains one of his most popular works.

Innovative Igor Stravinsky admired the more traditional Pyotr Ilyich Tchaikovsky, impressed both by his simplicity and his never-failing melody. Stravinsky and pianist Arthur Rubinstein were good friends. One evening, in parting, the world renowned composer astonished Rubinstein by declaring, "Ach, the devil. Sometimes I feel that everything I have done is a lot of rot."

Isn't that intriguing? Do you ever feel that way about your own life? I do. On the rare days when the mood is dour, I see my life as an endless cascade of flops and mistakes. Fortunately, this cloudy phase soon wanes, the cheery sun peeks through, and I resume being buoyant and happy to have led such a rich and diverse life.

It's then I recall how aspects of Utopia colored my days from the very beginning, when I was born into a community that expected the future to realize its hopes for an ideal life, the very definition of Utopia. Spontaneously, the thought came to me that I might be a spiritual teacher one day, an aspiration that was invoked in due time as I learned to meditate, had prized experiences of bubbling bliss, and subsequently taught the technique to several hundred people, some of whom were in pursuit of nirvana while others, also "seekers," were hot on the trail of sound sleep!

Mind you, the concept of Utopia dates back to a work in 1516 by Sir Thomas More that describes a perfect society on an imaginary or mythical island. More wrote his book in Latin and coined this new word, which translates as "no-place land," or "non-existing place." Utopia has since gained wide usage with connotations of something perfect, ideal, even heavenly.

In this light, Utopian fulfillment honored me on the worldly plane through various delightful avenues, ranging from the vocational via magazine work and a glossy writing career; to wondrous world travels and foreign sojourns with stimulating companions; and, finally, to a joyous appreciation of the sublime arts of poetry and music. Odd though that I should be so enraptured of everything melodious and yet be a total klutz at performing!

From music, let's return for a moment to film, where we have screen legends Joan Crawford and Bette Davis to consider. Fate plopped them both into the golden age of the cinema at the same time, then added a rebellious child to each household to complete the karmic crucible.

How do you feel about their mutual dilemma? Bette was inclined to be acerbic when dealing with Joan, but on publication of *Mommy Dearest,* Christina Crawford's rough assessment of her adoptive mother, she came to Joan's defense. Of course Joan was no longer living. Bette also spoke of how grateful she was to have a dutiful daughter of her own, not knowing what was in store. The daughter, B. D. Hyman, was about to bring out her unflattering account of Bette in a memoir entitled *My Mother's Keeper.*

I suspect these silver screen icons were tough to deal with, and I feel sympathy for the daughters. However, I wish they had dealt with their situation by confronting the mother directly rather than going public. Maybe they tried. They were served some hard lumps. Christina was pointedly left out of Joan's will, for example. That would not be easy to forget. I found the two books fascinating and quite well written.

Both daughters seem to be faring well these days, B.D. heading her television ministry and Christina with new editions of her book and campaigning for the reform of laws dealing with child abuse. Both have given us insights into the realities of home life involving glamorous parents and succeeded for once in upstaging their mothers, no mean feat. Perhaps that was a necessity for the young ladies. I wish them well.

I'm reflecting on my years in France when I say that in these matters I can switch easily from one side of a discussion to the other. The French, I found during my sojourn there, love to engage in philosophical disputes. Heated sessions in those legendary sidewalk cafes are commonplace. Sometimes, just when you think one fellow is about to clout the other, the two switch sides. At evening's end all clasp hands, hug, and swear eternal friendship. I recall one summer night when I entered a crowded, noisy café near the celebrated Sorbonne. As I made my way through, a patron, listening to the hum, gave me a big smile and said, "Il n'y a rien comme le baratin!" — There's nothing like good discourse, good chatter!

Are you a Francophile? An Anglophile? Any kind of phile? Although I was brought up speaking German and English, I have always felt completely at home in a French-speaking milieu. As so often, however, I bow in this instance to Maharishi, who loved his native India but never tired of saying in the ancient Sanskrit, *Vasu daiva kutumbakam* — "The world is my family."

This brings to mind one of the most wonderful passages in all of literature, the description in *The Ramayana,* the Indian epic, of what it was like to live in the age of the great ruler, Rama, a time thought to be legendary by some but viewed as a living reality by reputed historians.

> In the whole of Rama's realm there was no one who suffered from bodily pains, ill fortune, or evil circumstances. Every man loved his neighbor and, contented with the state of life to which he had been born, conformed to sound morality and the teaching of scripture.
>
> There was no sickness and no premature death. Everyone was trim and sound of body. No one was in poverty, in sorrow or in distress. No one was ignorant or unlucky. All men and women were naturally good and pious. Everyone was grateful for kindness and sincerely prudent.
>
> The trees in the forest were ever full of flowers and fruit. The elephant and the lion dwelt peacefully together... The cooing of the birds and the herds of deer fearlessly roaming the woods made a charming scene.
>
> The air was cool, fragrant, and splendidly mild. Bees laden with honey made a pleasant humming. Creepers and trees

yielded their sweetness on being asked. The earth was ever clothed with crops... Mines of jewels of every description were disclosed in the mountains and the world acknowledged its king to be in truth the Universal Spirit.

Every river flowed with the abundance of refreshing water — cool, pure, and delicious to the taste. The sea remained within its bounds, casting forth pearls on its shore for men to gather. The ponds were thick with lotuses, and every quarter of the world was supremely happy.

The moon flooded the earth with her radiance, the sun gave as much heat as was necessary, the clouds poured forth showers for the mere asking in the days when Rama was king.

This oft-cited quote is from the *Rama Charita Manasa,* a life of Rama by the great sage Tulsidas.

Don't you find that these words lift the spirit? This is also the glory of Maharishi, whose ever-present goal was to bring Enlightenment to all mankind and create a bright new golden age. Though he has departed, his teaching modalities are all in place.

There are many positive signs on the horizon despite the turmoil in parts of the world. Overall, major conflicts are apparently way down in recent decades. Significant crime categories are likewise on the wane. Environmentalists are launching trailblazing projects in many areas. Things may still look dark at times, the media obsessed with murder and mayhem, but eventually these negative tendencies will lose their grip. Keep looking for positive signs and I think you will find them in ever increasing numbers.

I must have told you that back in the 1970s Maharishi asked all of us on an advanced meditation course to go through the *New York Times* each day and make synopses of positive articles. Believe it or not, there were days when we could not find a single upbeat piece, save perhaps for a rousing sports score, but even that was always shadowed.

A friend of mine once came late to a Maharishi conference with the excuse that he was watching an exciting ballgame and couldn't tear himself away. "It was really great!" he concluded. "Oh," said Maharishi quietly, "nobody lost?" He was a great one for putting things in perspective.

Who do you look up to in this world? Who provides you with guidance, or solace, or joy? Is there some individual who offers all of these, someone about whom you have no reservations? You're very lucky if you've found such a sterling figure.

I'm off on a little trip so we won't be chatting for a few days. Meanwhile, give my love to almost anyone! — CIAO!

About the Author

NORMAN ZIEROLD was born in the Amana Colonies of southeast Iowa in 1927 and spent his young years in that simple, picturesque community until his enlistment in the United States Navy. The GI Bill of Rights then led Norman to Harvard, where he graduated cum laude, and on to the University of Iowa, where he earned a Master's Degree in English Literature.

Two halcyon years in Bordeaux and Paris on a French Government Teaching Assistantship were followed by an exciting decade in New York City where he taught at the prestigious Brearley School and served on *Collier's Encyclopedia* before landing rewarding assignments with *Theatre Arts Magazine* and *Show*.

Inevitably, as he had always planned, Norman began to write professionally. He has since published several books, including *Garbo, The Child Stars, The Moguls,* and *Sex Goddesses of the Silent Screen,* as well as two true-crime accounts, *Little Charley Ross* and *Three Sisters in Black,* which garnered a Special Edgar Allen Poe Award from the Mystery Writers of America.

Along the way, Norman met celebrities galore, including Barbara Walters, Andy Warhol, Mae West, Groucho Marx, Anaïs Nin, Tennessee Williams, Anthony Quinn, Rex Harrison, Shelley Winters, Carol Channing, and Jackie Coogan.

In 1972, Norman added a keystone to the arch of his life story, beginning the practice of Transcendental Meditation, which he found so personally satisfying that he became a teacher and taught the technique to many hundreds of people. Since 2002, Norman has been living in Fairfield, Iowa, where he works in the communications office at Maharishi University of Management.